[X] 空中乘务专业系列教材

应急设施与程序（第2版）

孙 芮　廖 曦 ◉ 编

西南交通大学出版社
·成 都·

图书在版编目（CIP）数据

应急设施与程序 / 孙芮，廖曦编. —2 版. —成都：西南交通大学出版社，2016.8（2024.1 重印）
空中乘务专业系列教材
ISBN 978-7-5643-4820-5

Ⅰ. ①应… Ⅱ. ①孙… ②廖… Ⅲ. ①民航运输 – 旅客运输 – 应急系统 – 教材 Ⅳ. ①F560.69

中国版本图书馆 CIP 数据核字（2016）第 168881 号

空中乘务专业系列教材
应急设施与程序
（第 2 版）
孙 芮 廖 曦 编

责 任 编 辑	赵玉婷
封 面 设 计	何东琳设计工作室
出 版 发 行	西南交通大学出版社
	（四川省成都市二环路北一段 111 号
	西南交通大学创新大厦 21 楼）
营 销 部 电 话	028-87600564　028-87600533
邮 政 编 码	610031
网　　　　址	http://www.xnjdcbs.com
印　　　　刷	成都蓉军广告印务有限责任公司
成 品 尺 寸	170 mm × 230 mm
印　　　　张	11
字　　　　数	253 千
版　　　　次	2016 年 8 月第 2 版
印　　　　次	2024 年 1 月第 4 次
书　　　　号	ISBN 978-7-5643-4820-5
定　　　　价	28.00 元

课件咨询电话：028-87600533
图书如有印装质量问题　本社负责退换
版权所有　盗版必究　举报电话：028-87600562

前　言

"应急设施与程序"是空中乘务专业的核心课程。该课程的目的是通过学习，使学生熟悉并能操作飞机客舱的应急设施，熟悉并能实施各种情况下的应急程序。因此，该课程为理论与实践结合课，尤其注重实践技能的培养。本教材以目前的大众机型 A320 飞机为蓝本，对客舱内应急设施的位置、功能、使用方法、应急情况下的处置程序作了详细的介绍。考虑到该课程的特点和学生的英语水平，编排时我们以节为单位列出了困难的单词，并加注音标和汉语释义，同时为检查阅读理解设计了相关问题。该教材由中国民航飞行学院空乘学院孙芮、廖曦编写。陈艾莎教授对全书进行了审阅。

编　者
2013 年 4 月

TABLE OF CONTENTS

PART I EMERGENCY EQUIPMENT

CHAPTER 1 PORTABLE EMERGENCY EQUIPMENT ········ 3

- Section 1   Location ········ 3
- Section 2   First Aid Kit ········ 9
- Section 3   Flashlight ········ 11
- Section 4   Megaphone ········ 15
- Section 5   Emergency Radio Beacon ········ 16
- Section 6   Portable Fire Extinguisher ········ 22
- Section 7   Portable Oxygen Cylinder ········ 26
- Section 8   Portable Breathing Equipment ········ 30
- Section 9   Life Vest ········ 33
- Section 10 Life Raft ········ 37
- Section 11 Portable Emergency Equipment in the Cockpit ········ 42

CHAPTER 2 FIXED EMERGENCY EQUIPMENT ········ 46

- Section 1   Emergency Locator Transmitter System (ELT System) ········ 46
- Section 2   Doors and Exits in the Cabin ········ 49
- Section 3   Slide Rafts ········ 59
- Section 4   Life Lines ········ 65
- Section 5   Passenger Emergency Oxygen System ········ 67
- Section 6   Lavatory Fire Extinguish System ········ 71
- Section 7   Emergency Lighting System ········ 75

PART II EMERGENCY PROCEDURES

CHAPTER 3   GENERAL INFORMATION FOR IN-FLIGHT EMERGENCY ········ 81

CHAPTER 4   INFLIGHT EMERGENCY ········ 85
- Section 1   Turbulence ········ 85
- Section 2   Slow Air Leaks ········ 90
- Section 3   Cabin Decompression ········ 92
- Section 4   Cabin Smoke ········ 99
- Section 5   Fire Prevention Awareness ········ 102
- Section 6   Area Specific Fires ········ 108
- Section 7   Bomb and Sabotage Threats ········ 115
- Section 8   Hijacking ········ 119

CHAPTER 5   EMERGENCY EVACUATIONS ········ 123
- Section 1   Introduction ········ 123
- Section 2   Unplanned Ground Evacuation ········ 126
- Section 3   Planned Ground Evacuation ········ 131
- Section 4   Ditching ········ 143
- Section 5   Commands ········ 151
- Section 6   Flight Attendant Jump Seats and Exit Responsibilities ········ 152

CHAPTER 6   SURVIVAL ········ 156

REFERENCES ········ 169

PART I

EMERGENCY EQUIPMENT

PART I *EMERGENCY EQUIPMENT*

CHAPTER 1 PORTABLE EMERGENCY EQUIPMENT

Section 1 Location

The portable emergency equipment is stowed or installed at different locations throughout the whole aircraft, for instance, in the galley area, in the attendant seats area, in the overhead stowage or in the cabin stowage. They provide promotion to the cabin crew during emergency.

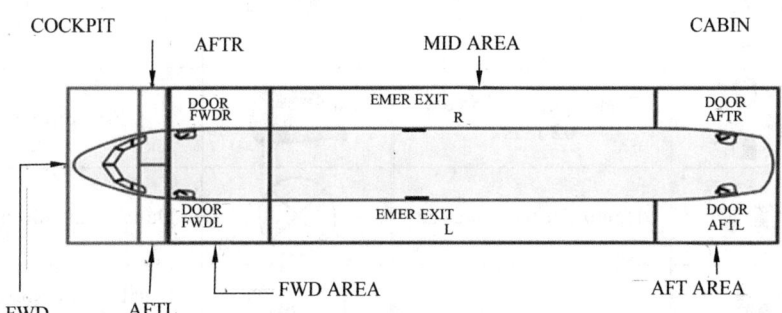

Figure 1.1 Location of the Portable Emergency Equipment

The following symbol table and the added graphics give an overview about the type and the location of these parts.

SYMBOL TABLE

SYMBOL	TITLE	SYMBOL	TITLE
	02 kit: 02 bottle 02 mask	R	Respirator
	Breathing hood	CS	Child seat

SYMBOL TABLE

SYMBOL	TITLE	SYMBOL	TITLE
	Life vest/jacket–cabin crew(one stowed under each C/A seat) Life vest/jacket–flight crew (stowed in cockpit)	BC	Baby cot
	Life vest–passenger (one stowed under each seat or in box under armrest)		Crash axe
	Spare life vest/jacket		Crow bar
	Infant life vest/jacket		Escape rope
	Survival raft		Life line
	Demo pack: life vest 02 mask Demo belt		Flashlight
	Demo pack: life vest 02 mask		Fire gloves
	Demo life vest/jacket		Dangerous goods kit
	Megaphone	DPSH	Disabled person seat harness
	Hazard Tape	H	Fire extinguisher (Halon)
	Crew tabard	W	Fire extinguisher (water)
	Radio beacon	PAX	Spare seat belt
S	Survival kit	INF	Infant seat belt

PART | *EMERGENCY EQUIPMENT*

SYMBOL TABLE

SYMBOL	TITLE	SYMBOL	TITLE
✚	First aid kit	EXT	Extension belt
D	Defibrillator	SM	Security mirror
F	Fire fighting kit	△	Manual release tool

The table above shows all symbols which are used to identify the installed portable emergency equipment. Depending on the airlines' choices and/or airworthiness requirements, some of these items may be not installed on this aircraft. The location of the installed portable emergency equipment at delivery of this aircraft is shown below.

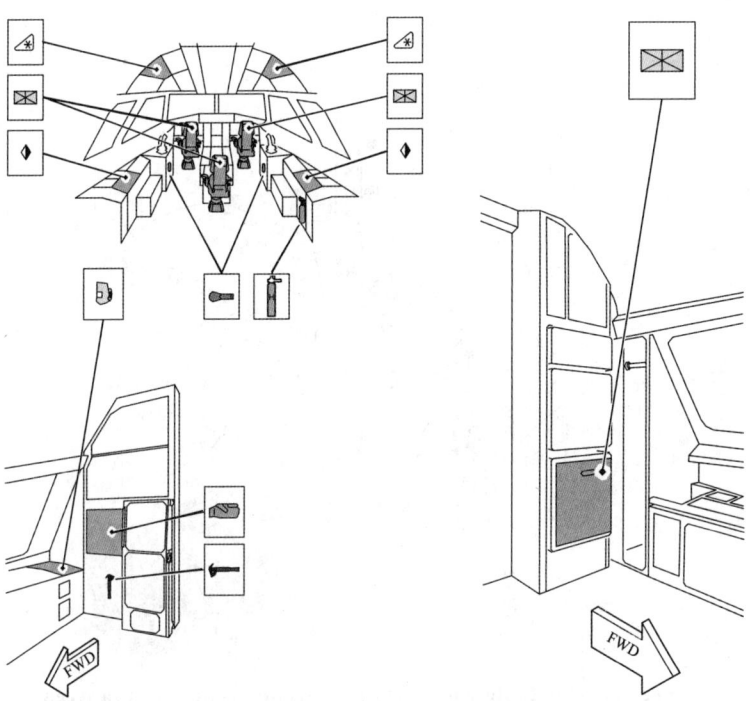

Figure 1.2   Portable Emergency Equipment–Cockpit

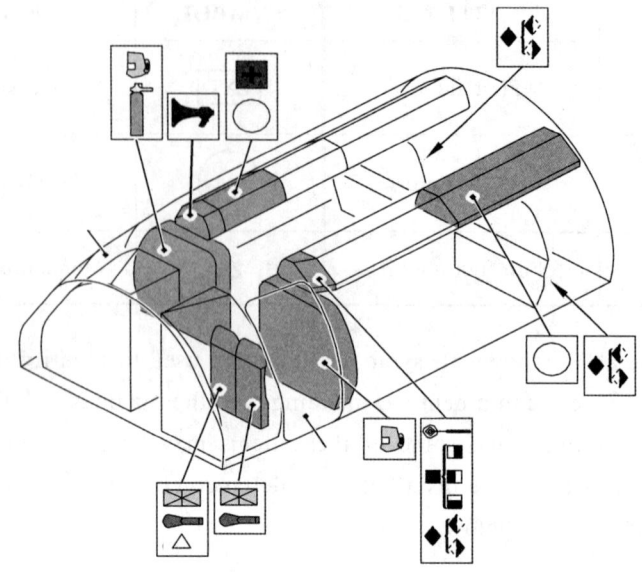

Figure 1.3　Portable Emergency Equipment–Fwd Cabin Area

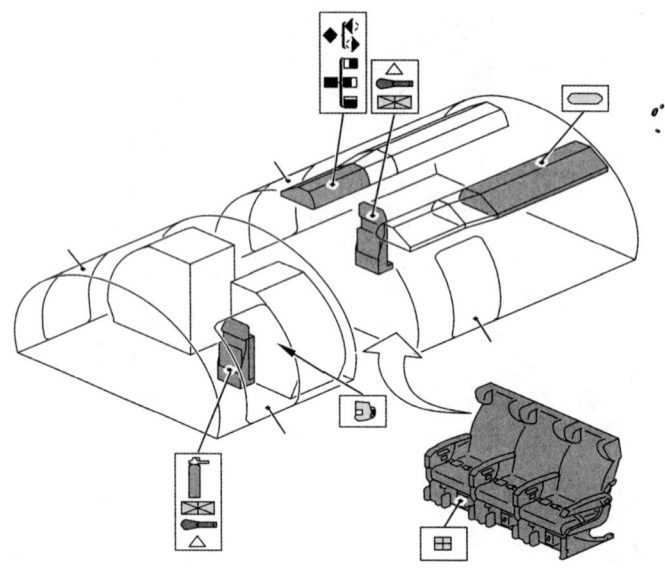

Figure 1.4　Portable Emergency Equipment–Mid Cabin Area

PART I *EMERGENCY EQUIPMENT*

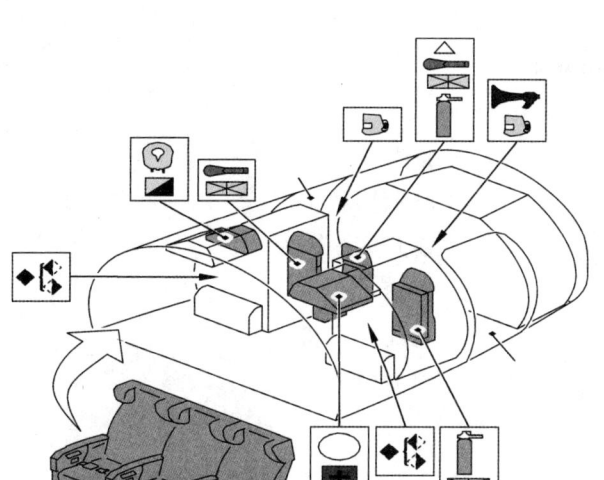

Figure 1.5　Portable Emergency Equipment–Aft Cabin Area

Words and Expressions

portable ['pɔ:təbl]　　*adj.* 便于携带的；手提式的
stow [stəʊ]　　*vt.* 装载
respirator ['respə,reɪtə]　　*n.* 呼吸器
hood [hʊd]　　*n.* 帽状物（烟囱帽、灯罩等）；头罩
megaphone ['megə,fəʊn]　　*n.* 扩音器
harness ['hɑ:nɪs]　　*n.* 马具，挽具
extinguisher [ɪk'stɪŋgwɪʃə]　　*n.* 消火器，熄火器，灭火器
tabard ['tæbəd]　　*n.* 无袖短外套
beacon ['bi:kən]　　*n.* 无线电台或发射台；信号站
extension [ɪks'tenʃən]　　*n.* 延伸，扩展；增加部分
defibrillator [di:'fɪbrɪleɪtə]　　*n.* （电击）除颤器
manual ['mænjʊəl]　　*adj.* 用手的，手工的
　　　　　　　　　　　n. 手册，指南
survival [sə'vaɪvəl]　　*n.* 幸存，生存；幸存者；残存物
raft [rɑ:ft]　　*n.* 筏，桴，木排

Technical Terms

life vest	救生衣
demo life vest	演示用救生衣
baby cot	婴儿床
crow bar	撬棒
radio beacon	无线发报机
survival kit	救命包

Notes

1. The portable emergency equipment is stowed or installed at different locations throughout the whole aircraft. 便携应急设备储藏并安装在整架飞机不同的位置。
2. The table above shows all symbols which are used to identify the installed portable emergency equipment. 上面的表格是机上便携式应急设备相对应的符号标识。
3. Depending on the airlines' choices and/or airworthiness requirements some of these items are maybe not installed on this aircraft. 根据航空公司或者适航要求，机上的某些应急设备可能没有安装。

Exercises

Please answer the following questions.

1. According to the text, find out the general locations of portable emergency equipment.
2. What are the symbols used to identify the installed portable emergency equipment?
3. If the flight attendant wants to check out the emergency equipment location, what should he/she do?

PART Ⅰ　*EMERGENCY EQUIPMENT*

Section 2　First Aid Kit

A first aid kit is a collection of supplies and equipment for use in giving first aid and can put together for the purpose (by an individual or organization, for instance), or purchased complete.

Usually there must be at least one first aid kit on board the aircraft. Maybe there is no first aid kit installed at the day of aircraft delivery; however, the airline is responsible to install the first aid kit(s) before operating the aircraft.

Each first aid kit should be installed on certain place; it is recommended that all kits are in a clean, waterproof container to keep the contents safe and aseptic. Kits should also be checked regularly and restocked if any items are damaged or expired. Each has a content list inside, which includes bandage, triangular bandages, alcohol rub, medical glove, adhesive bandages, scissors, etc.

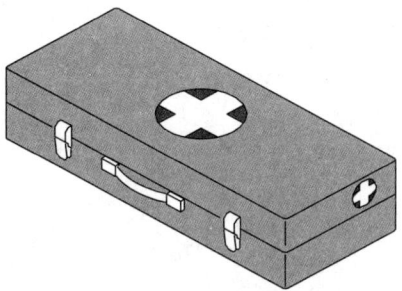

Figure 1.6

It should be used for traumas on board. Only those who are specifically trained and/or the on-the-spot medical personnel or other people who are well trained can use this kit. However, the off-duty flight attendants can use it only when they can improve his or her identity. After using, it should be documented for two copies: one is for the purse or the captain; one is required to put into the kit which will be handed into the medical center.

Words and Expressions

waterproof ['wɔ:təpru:f]　　*adj.* 不透水的，防水的；用防水材料处理过的

aseptic [əˈseptɪk]　　*adj.* <术>无菌的；经消毒的；防感染的；冷漠的
expire [ɪksˈpaɪə]　　*vi.* 期满；文件、协议等（因到期而）失效
bandage [ˈbændɪdʒ]　　*n.* 绷带
triangular [traɪˈæŋɡjələ]　　*adj.* 三角（形）的
adhesive [ədˈhiːsɪv]　　*n.* 黏合剂，粘着剂
　　　　　　　　　　　adj. 可黏着的，黏性的
scissor [ˈsɪzə]　　*vt.* （用剪刀）剪；作剪式移动（尤指腿）
trauma [ˈtraʊmə]　　*n.* 创伤；损伤；挫折
document [ˈdɒkjumənt]　　*n.* 文档，证件
　　　　　　　　　　　vt. 证明；记录；为……提供证明

Technical Terms

first aid kit	急救箱
triangular bandage	三角巾
alcohol rub	酒精擦
medical glove	医用橡胶手套
adhesive bandage	创可贴

Notes

1. It is recommended that all kits are in a clean, waterproof container to keep the contents safe and aseptic. 建议急救箱物品放置在干净防水的盒子里，以保持物品的安全性，防止污染。
2. Kits should also be checked regularly and restocked if any items are damaged or expired. 定期检查急救箱，如果有任何物品损坏或过期，应及时更换。
3. Only those who are specifically trained and/or the on-the-spot medical personnel or other people who are well trained can use this kit. 只有那些经过专门训练的，或者在场的医务人员，或者其他训练有素的人员可以使用急救箱。

PART Ⅰ EMERGENCY EQUIPMENT

Exercises

Please answer the following questions.

1. What does the first aid kit consist of?
2. Who is qualified to use the first aid kit?
3. Is the first aid kit available to anyone on board the aircraft? Why?

Section 3 Flashlight

Flashlight Cabin

A lot of flashlights are installed throughout the aircraft. The flashlight is explosion proof and powered by dry batteries. The flashlight is ON automatically, when removed from the retention bracket. The flashlight is OFF automatically, when put into the retention bracket.

To remove the flashlight from the retaining clip, one should hold the body of the flashlight, and then pull it from the retaining clip of the retention bracket; the tamper shield will be disconnected.

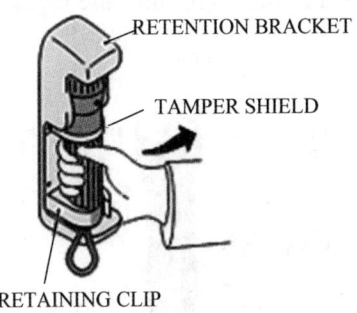

Figure 1.7

To install the flashlight back, one should hold the body of the flashlight, noting that the fin has to point to the retention bracket and the LED has to point away from the retention bracket. Then let the fins of the flashlight move into the recess of the retention bracket. At last, push the body of the flashlight into the retaining clip.

Flashlight Cockpit

The flashlight is powered by 2 alkaline manganese dioxide batteries. The main components of the flashlight are: a body, a reflector assembly, a lens, a switch assembly, with button and cap.

A cracked or broken flashlight bulb that remains glowing has the potential to cause an explosion in hazardous atmospheres.

The flashlight is usable for constant light and impulse light. For constant light, slide back the cap of the switch assembly, firmly press the button until it engages, the light comes on. For impulse light, slide back the cap, firmly press the button until it engages, the light comes on; light pressing on the button lets the light goes off and releasing the button, let the light comes on again.

The S.O.S.signal can be transmitted by the flashlight. The S.O.S.signal is three times a short signal (for S), three times a long signal (for O), and three times a short signal (for S). To operate, firmly pressing the button until it disengages; the light goes off, sliding back the cap of the switch assembly; firmly pushing the body of the flashlight into the bracket.

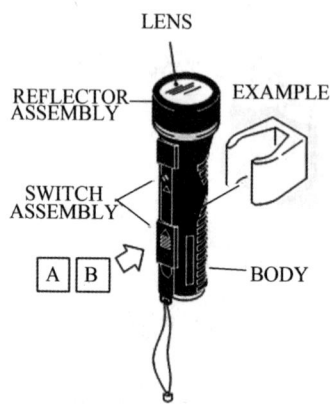

Figure 1.8

PART I EMERGENCY EQUIPMENT

Words and Expressions

automatically [ˌɔ:tə'mætɪkəlɪ]   *adv.* 自动地，机械地
retention [rɪ'tenʃən]   *n.* 挡住，拦阻；保持，保留，容纳
bracket ['brækɪt]   *n.* 壁架，托架；括弧
retain [rɪ'teɪn]   *vt.* 保持；保留；止住；容纳
clip [klɪp]   *n.* 夹子，回纹针，别针
tamper ['tæmpə]   *vt.* 窜改；瞎摆弄；瞎搞；玩弄
fin [fɪn]   *n.* 鳍，鱼翅；鳍状物；汽车尾部的突起装饰物
LED   *abbr.* light-emitting diode 发光二级管
recess [rɪ'ses]   *n.* （墙壁、山脉等的）凹进处（部分），凹口（座、槽）；壁龛
alkaline ['ælkəlɪn, -ˌlaɪn]   *adj.* 碱的，碱性的
manganese ['mæŋgəˌni:z, -ˌni:s]   *n.* 〈化〉锰
dioxide [daɪ'ɒksaɪd]   *n.* [化]二氧化物
reflector [rɪ'flektə]   *n.* 反射器；反射光（热、声音）的物体
assembly [ə'semblɪ]   *n.* 集合；集会；部件，组（合）件；成套件；联合装置
lens [lenz]   *n.* 透镜；（凹、凸）镜片；一组透镜
bulb [bʌlb]   *n.* 玻璃泡；灯泡
glow [gləʊ]   *vt.* 发白热光，灼热；发光（热）
hazardous ['hæzədəs]   *adj.* 危险的，冒险的
constant ['kɒnstənt]   *adj.* 经常的，稳定的，不断的
impulse ['ɪmpʌls]   *n.* 推动，冲力，刺激，推动力
engage [ɪn'geɪdʒ]   *vt. & vi.* （使）从事于，（使）忙于；吸引，占用
sequence ['si:kwəns]   *n.* 先后次序，顺序，连续

Technical Terms

alkaline manganese dioxide battery　　　碱性锰电池
constant light　　　连续/持续光照

impulse light	脉冲光
reflector assembly	反射组件
switch assembly	开关组件

Notes

1. The flashlight is powered by 2 alkaline manganese dioxide batteries. 手电筒是由两节碱性锰电池提供光源。
2. A cracked or broken flashlight bulb that remains glowing has the potential to cause an explosion in hazardous atmospheres. 有裂纹或者破损的灯泡，如果在危险的环境下持续发光，有可能造成爆炸。
3. The flashlight is usable for constant light and impulse light. 手电筒可以提供连续光和脉冲光两种形式的光照。
4. The S.O.S. signal can be transmitted by the flashlight. 可以使用手电筒来发送 SOS 信号。

注：S.O.S.是国际莫尔斯电码救难信号，并非任何单词的缩写，但也有很多人认为是"save our souls 拯救我们的灵魂"的意思。20 世纪初，海难事件频繁发生，由于不能及时发出求救信号和最快组织施救，造成很大的人员伤亡和财产损失。鉴于此，国际无线电报公约组织于 1908 年正式将它确定为国际通用海难求救信号。其实这三个字母的组合没有任何实际意义，只是因为它的电码"…---…"在电报中是发报方最容易发出，接报方最容易辨识的电码。

Exercises

Please answer the following questions.

1. What are the features and operation of the flashlight on board?
2. How is the S.O.S. signal made by using a flashlight?
3. What are the main differences between two kinds of flashlights on board?

PART I *EMERGENCY EQUIPMENT*

Section 4　Megaphone

A megaphone is a portable, usually hand-held, cone-shaped horn used to amplify a person's voice or other sounds towards a targeted direction. The on-board megaphones are powered by 8 alkaline batteries (AA-size) each, with a mouthpiece and a push-button switch.

Here is the operation of the megaphone. Hold the megaphone to the mouth. But do not place the hand around the mouthpiece. Point the megaphone towards the passengers. Do not point it to the bulkhead. When the natural human voice is sent through a megaphone, the sound is concentrated in a given direction and the coupling of its energy to the air is optimized, while if a listener is to the side, it is more difficult to hear what is being said. Do not operate the megaphone near a person's ears, amplified sound or howling can cause damage to the inner ear. Contact the mouthpiece of the megaphone with the lips. Push the push-button switch and then speak slowly with a strong voice so that it can be heard clearly.

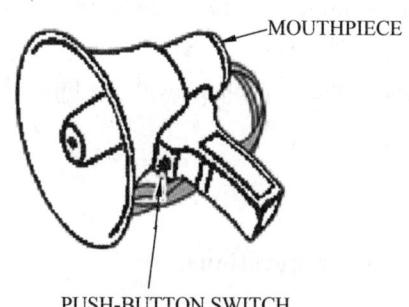

Figure 1.9

Words and Expressions

amplify ['æmplɪfaɪ]　　*vt.* 放大，扩大，增强
howling ['haʊlɪŋ]　　*n.* 啸声，嚎鸣
couple ['kʌpl]　　*vt.&vi.* 连在一起，连接
optimize ['ɒptɪˌmaɪz]　　*v.* 使最优化，使尽可能有效

Technical Terms

the inner ear   内耳
bulkhead   舱壁，隔板

Notes

1. A megaphone is a portable, usually hand-held, cone-shaped horn used to amplify a person's voice or other sounds towards a targeted direction. 机上扩音器是一种便携式设备，可直接手持，呈锥型喇叭状，用来将人的声音或者其他声音放大到一个既定的方向。
2. When the natural human voice is sent through a megaphone, the sound is concentrated in a given direction and the coupling of its energy to the air is optimized. 当人的自然发音通过扩音器，声音就会集中到一个固定的方向，以优化的音质呈现。
3. Amplified sound or howling can cause damage to the inner ear. 放大的声音或者嚎叫声会损伤人的内耳。
4. Contact the mouthpiece of the megaphone with the lips. 让嘴唇接触到送话器。

Exercises

Please answer the following questions.

1. How does the megaphone function on board the aircraft?
2. What should be paid attention to during the use of the megaphone?
3. What are the suggestions from your personal experience when using the megaphone in a limited space?

Section 5   Emergency Radio Beacon

Most commercial aircrafts are required to carry an ELT (emergency locator

PART | EMERGENCY EQUIPMENT

transmitter). The beacon transmits distress signals simultaneously on three frequencies: 121.5 MHz for civil distress frequency, 243 MHz for military distress frequency and 406.025 MHz COSPAS-SARSAT frequency.

There are two types of ELT.

One is a compact, buoyant emergency locator transmitter with an identification plate, an operating instruction plate, a battery plate, an electronic assembly, a float, an antenna, and a lanyard.

The emergency radio beacon (referred to as the beacon) operates in water or on land. Operating instructions are given on the operating-instruction plate bonded on the beacon's housing.

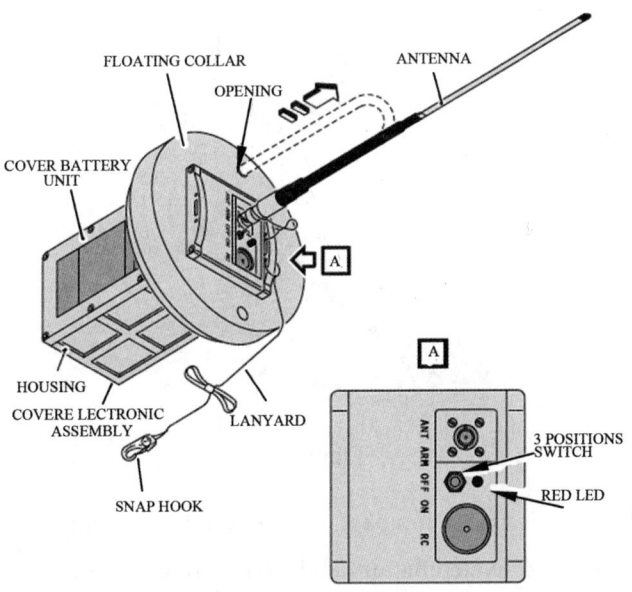

Figure 1.10

When the beacon is operated in water, unwind the lanyard beginning with the snap hook, and then connect the snap hook with the lanyard securely to the raft. After that, carefully pull the antenna from the opening and position the antenna, activate the beacon by switching the beacon's ARM/OFF/ON 3-position-switch to the ON position. This switch is placed on the front face of the electronic assembly. At last, put the emergency radio beacon into the water. The emergency radio beacon operates automatically in a few seconds and drifts out to the end of the lanyard.

When the beacon is operated on land, look for an area clear of obstruction such as trees, and choose the highest point for best transmission. Then carefully pull the antenna from the opening and position the antenna, activate the beacon by switching the beacon's 3-position-switch to the ON position. This switch is placed on the front face of the electronic assembly and place the beacon properly. The emergency radio beacon operates automatically in a few seconds.

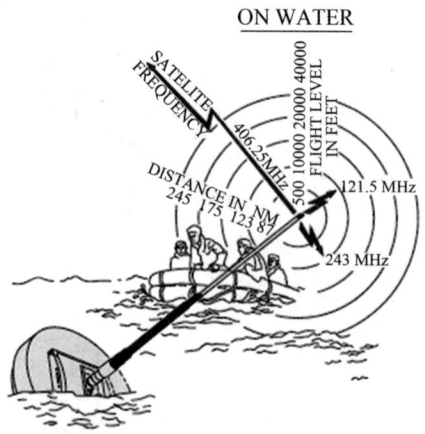

Figure 1.11

The other type is also a compact, buoyant, automatic unit, which consists of an antenna, a water-activated battery and a triple frequency antenna.

It is a water-activated survival ELT. When activated by immersing in a suitable liquid, the ELT provides a homing signal for civil and military search aircraft and satellites. ELT has a polyethylene liquid container wrapped around the body of the battery casing. The liquid container may be used to contain salt-water or other suitable fluid for activating the battery under abnormal conditions such as a non liquid sea water environment.

PART I *EMERGENCY EQUIPMENT*

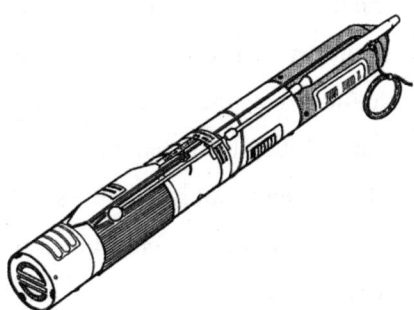

Figure 1.12

When the ELT is immersed in water, the battery is activated by the salt-water entering through holes in the battery casing. The antenna is automatically erected from its stowed position upon immersion. The antenna may also be manually deployed. The water-soluble tape, securing the cord assembly, is softened in approximately 30 seconds of immersion in water. It allows the ELT to drift up to 60 feet (18.3 m) from the raft or boat. The cord may also be manually released by breaking the tape.

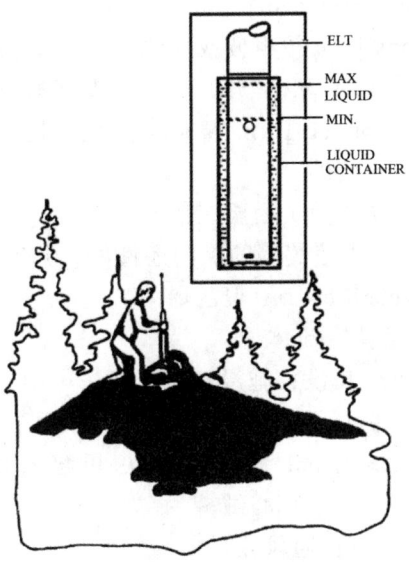

Figure 1.13

The ELT can also manually be deployed on land. If on land, move ELT to an area clear of obstructions, such as dense forest, and select the highest point for best transmission. One should break the tape, hold the antenna and allow the antenna to erect, and then unroll the plastic bag under the cord, insert the lower end into the plastic bag, make sure the solution covers the two vent holes located at side of ELT at all times. To temporarily interrupt transmission, remove ELT from water or liquid container and invert.

Words and Expressions

housing ['haʊzɪŋ]　*n.* 外壳，外罩
compact [kəm'pækt]　*adj.* 装填紧密的，整齐填满的
buoyant ['bɔɪənt, 'bu:jənt]　*adj.* 有浮力的，容易复原的
antenna [æn'tenə]　*n.* 触角，触须；天线
lanyard ['lænjəd]　*n.*（船上系物用的）短索；安全绳
distress [dɪs'tres]　*n.* 危难，不幸
　　　　　　　　　　 vt. 使痛苦，使忧伤
simultaneously [ˌsaɪməl'teɪnɪəsli]　*adv.* 同时地
frequency ['fri:kwənsi]　*n.*（声波或无线电波的）振动频率；波段
unwind [ʌn'waɪnd]　*vt. & vi.* 解开，展开（卷绕的东西）；伸直
obstruction [əb'strʌkʃən, ɔb-]　*n.* 障碍物，阻碍物；阻碍，阻挠
triple ['trɪpl]　*adj.* 三倍的
　　　　　　　 vt. & vi.（使）增至三倍
homing ['həʊmɪŋ]　*n.*（信鸽等的）归还性能；归航；自动引导
polyethylene [ˌpɔlɪ'eθəli:n]　*n.* 聚乙烯
fluid ['flu:ɪd]　*n.* 液体，流体
immerse [ɪ'mɜ:s]　*vt.* 浸没；施浸礼；沉迷……中，陷入
deploy [dɪ'plɔɪ]　*vt. & vi.*（尤指军事行动）使展开；施展；有效地利用
water-soluble ['wɔ:təˌsɔljəbəl, 'wɔtə-]　*adj.* 可溶于水的
cord [kɔ:d]　*n.*（细）绳；灯心绒裤
vent [vent]　*n.* 孔，口；通风孔
invert [ɪn'vɜ:t]　*vt.* 使……前后倒置；使反转

PART Ⅰ *EMERGENCY EQUIPMENT*

Technical Terms

emergency locator transmitter	应急发报机
identification plate	识别面板
electronic assembly	电子组件
water-activated battery	海水电池
battery casing	电池盒
distress signal	遇难信号
battery plate	蓄电池极板
snap hook	安全挂钩
MHz (*abbr.* megahertz)	兆赫[兹]

Notes

1. The beacon transmits distress signals simultaneously on three frequencies. 发报机会同时发射出三种频率的求救信号。

2. Operating instructions are given on the operating-instruction plate bonded on the beacon's housing. 在发报机外壳的操作面板上附有操作说明。

3. Pull the antenna from the opening and position the antenna, activate the beacon by switching the beacon's ARM/OFF/ON 3-position-switch to the ON position. 将天线从插口取出后拔直，再将发报机控制面板上的三档开关调到 ON 的位置，发报机开始工作。

4. The emergency radio beacon operates automatically in a few seconds and drifts out to the end of the lanyard. 几秒钟以后发报机自动开始工作，然后慢慢漂移开。

5. To temporarily interrupt transmission, remove ELT from water or liquid container and invert. 要临时中止发报，将发报机从水中或者装有液体的容器中取出，再将其倒置。

Exercises

Please answer the following questions.

1. What are the frequencies the beacon transmits distress signals simultaneously?
2. What is the main feature of ELT?
3. What are the differences between the two types of ELT?
4. What should be paid attention to when operating an ELT on land?
5. How do you operate an ELT in water?

Section 6　Portable Fire Extinguisher

A fire extinguisher, flame extinguisher, or simply an extinguisher, is an active fire protection device used to extinguish or control small fires, often in emergency situations.

The portable fire extinguisher is filled with Halon 1211 and extinguishes small fires as such its capacity is limited. The fire extinguisher is pressurized with nitrogen to get the force that is necessary to push the extinguishing agent from the cylinder. The extinguishing agent and the nitrogen are kept in the cylinder by the valve assembly until the lever is manually operated.

To operate, one should remove the portable fire extinguisher from the bracket, read the Instruction, Cautions and Warnings bonded on the fire extinguishers bottle. Carry the extinguisher by holding it on the carrying handle. Hold the extinguisher upright and lift the handle, bend down the safe guard and remove the seal wire. The user should stand at least 1.8 m (6 ft.) away from the fire, aim the nozzle at the base of flame, and depress the trigger to start the flow of extinguishant.

PART Ⅰ *EMERGENCY EQUIPMENT*

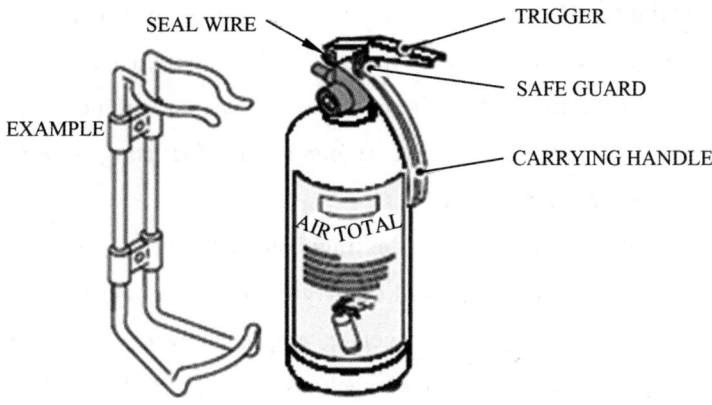

Figure 1.14

It is recommended to use a smoke hood when fighting a fire. Smoke from fire and gas from the fire extinguisher may cause irritation of the eyes and respiratory organs.

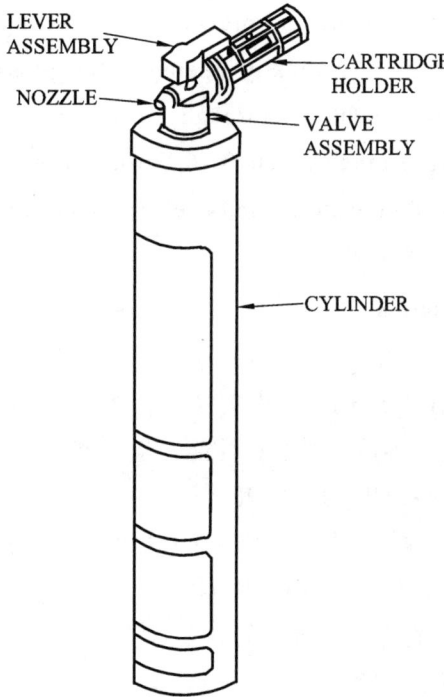

Figure 1.15

In the cockpit, a Halon 1211 portable fire extinguisher is also available. The instruction for operation of the fire extinguisher is shown on a placard bonded on the body of the extinguisher. The fire extinguisher has a monoblock pressed steel tank, red coated, a valve tap with a trigger handle for using a carriage and a jet-spray. The content is Halon 1211.

Besides Halon portable fire extinguisher, there is another kind of extinguisher installed in the aircraft–liquid-type fire extinguisher. The cylinder is filled with a solution of potassium acetate, ethylene-glycol, and water. A valve assembly is installed on the cylinder neck. A cartridge holder, a nozzle and a lever assembly are attached to the valve assembly. A lock ring and a seal wire are installed on the cartridge holder to prevent accidental arming and discharge of the fire extinguisher.

When the cartridge holder is turned clockwise, which is shown by the arrow label on the cartridge holder, the piercing pin assembly ruptures the cartridge. This releases the carbon dioxide and pressurizes the extinguishing agent in the cylinder. When the lever is manually operated, the pressure in the cylinder pushes the extinguishing agent out through the nozzle. The discharge time is about 45 seconds, with a range of 20 ft (6.1 m). It cools burning material by absorbing heat from burning material and is effective on Class A fires.

Words and Expressions

extinguish [ɪksˈtɪŋgwɪʃ]　　*vt.* 熄灭（火）

capacity [kəˈpæsɪti]　　*n.* 容量；才能；性能；生产能力

nitrogen [ˈnaɪtrədʒən]　　*n.* [化]氮，氮气

cylinder [ˈsɪlɪndə]　　*n.* 圆筒，圆柱；汽缸；（尤指用作容器的）圆筒状物

lever [ˈli:və]　　*n.* 杆；杠杆，类似杠杆的物体

upright [ˈʌpraɪt]　　*adj.* 直立的；垂直的

nozzle [ˈnɒzəl]　　*n.* 管嘴，喷嘴

trigger [ˈtrɪgə]　　*n.* 扳柄；闸柄；制动器；制滑机；锁定装置

PART Ⅰ *EMERGENCY EQUIPMENT*

irritation [ˌɪrɪ'teɪʃən]   *n.* 激怒；恼怒；生气；令人恼火的事；疼痛处；疼痛感
respiratory ['respərətrɪ, -ˌtɔːrɪ, rɪ'spaɪərə-]   *adj.* 呼吸的，呼吸用的
placard ['plæk,ɑrd, -əd]   *n.* 招贴，布告；标语牌；海报
monoblock ['mɒnəʊˌblɒk]   *n.* 单块
coat [kəʊt]   *vt.* 覆盖……的表面
solution [sə'luːʃən]   *n.* 解决；溶解；溶液；答案
potassium [pə'tæsiːəm]   *n.* <化>钾
acetate ['æsɪˌtet]   *n.* 醋酸纤维；醋酸人造丝
ethylene ['eθɪliːn]   *n.* 乙烯
glycol ['glaɪkɔl]   *n.* 乙二醇
cartridge ['kɑːtrɪdʒ]   *n.* 子弹，弹药筒；暗盒，胶卷盒
rupture ['rʌptʃə]   *vt.& vi.* 使破裂；断绝（关系等）
discharge [dɪs'tʃɑːdʒ]   *vt.& vi.* 放出；流出；开枪；发射
piercing ['pɪəsɪŋ]   *adj.* 刺骨的；锐利的；锋利的

Technical Terms

portable fire extinguisher	便携式灭火瓶
safe guard	安全销
seal wire	铅封
trigger lever	触发器
smoke hood	防烟面罩
potassium acetate	乙酸钾
ethylene glycol	乙二醇
discharge outlet	出水口；排水出路

Notes

1. A fire extinguisher, flame extinguisher, or simply an extinguisher, is an active fire protection device used to extinguish or control small fires, often in emergency situations.
机上灭火器是紧急情况下用来熄灭或控制机上火灾的设备。

2. The portable fire extinguisher is filled with Halon 1211 and extinguishes small fires as such its capacity is limited.

便携式灭火器的灭火剂为 Halon 1211，由于容量有限，适用于小型火情。

3. The fire extinguisher has a monoblock pressed steel tank, red coated, a valve tap with a trigger handle for using a carriage and a jet-spray and the content is Halon 1211.

灭火器为红色单体钢瓶，阀门由把手、触发器和喷嘴组成，充装了 Halon 1211 灭火剂。

4. When the cartridge holder is turned clockwise, which is shown by the arrow label on the cartridge holder, the piercing pin assembly ruptures the cartridge.

按照手柄上的剪头方向顺时针旋转把手，可以拧断铅封。

Exercises

Ⅰ. Please answer the following questions.

1. Restate the operation of the portable fire extinguisher in the cabin.
2. What's the difference between the portable fire extinguisher in cockpit and that in cabin?

Ⅱ. Focusing on Practice

Objective:

　　Master the use of the portable fire extinguisher in the cabin.

Suggestions:

　　Practice can be fullfilled through grouping in the class. All the process should be timed by the group leader or the instructor.

Section 7　Portable Oxygen Cylinder

　　Two independent emergency oxygen systems are provided, one for the flight

PART I EMERGENCY EQUIPMENT

crew and one for the passengers. Portable oxygen cylinders are located in the cabin for emergency use.

The portable oxygen system is a self-contained breathing system offering demand, pressure-demand and constant flow capabilities. It provides high efficiency supplementary oxygen and respiratory protection for aviation use. It has two constant flow outlets, a relief valve protecting the low-pressure system from over-pressurization, a fingertip controlled ON-OFF valve, a pressure gauge indicating oxygen supply, a high-pressure safety relief device, a demand or pressure-demand regulator, a carrying strap, and a soft rubber-like oral-nasal mask with the flow indicator assembly. The demand and pressure-demand regulators operate with the smoke mask to protect the crew. It is lightweight and easy to operate. The cylinder capacities range from 4.3 to 48.3 cubic feet.

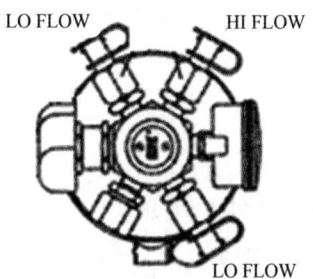

Figure 1.16

A portable oxygen cylinder assembly installed on the flight deck provides for supplemental breathing when required. The portable oxygen cylinder assembly has a shutoff valve, a pressure gauge and a disposable continuous flow mask.

When using, place the portable tank on a stable surface to prevent it from tipping or falling, and ensure that the unit is away from heat sources, such as ovens or heaters. Oxygen is flammable, using oxygen or transporting the oxygen tank near open flames is not acceptable. It is also not allowed to smoke during oxygen administration or near smoking devices. Improper use may result in serious injury or death. This equipment is intended to be used only for aviation applications and is to be used only by or under the supervision of a crew member trained and qualified.

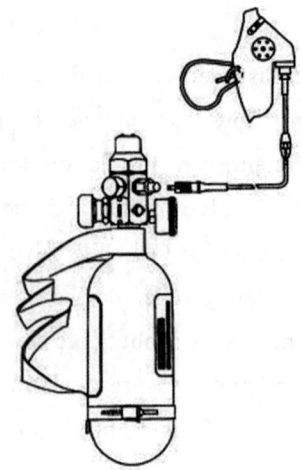

Figure 1.17

Words and Expressions

demand [dɪ'mɑːnd]　　*vt. & vi.* 要求，请求
　　　　　　　　　　n. 需求；需要
supplementary [ˌsʌplɪ'mentərɪ]　　*adj.* 增补的，追加的
outlet ['aʊtlet]　　*n.* 出口，出路；排水口，通风口
gauge [geɪdʒ]　　*n.* 测量的标准或范围；尺度
fingertip ['fɪŋɡəˌtɪp]　　*n.* 指尖；指套
strap [stræp]　　*n.* 带子；皮带；磨刀皮带；鞭打
assembly [ə'semblɪ]　　*n.* 装配；集会
disposable [dɪ'spəʊzəbəl]　　*adj.* 一次性的，可任意处理的；用后就抛弃的
flammable ['flæməbəl]　　*adj.* 易燃的，可燃的
tip [tɪp]　　*vt. & vi.* 给小费；倾斜，翻倒；装顶端
transport [træns'pɔːt]　　*vt.* 运送，运输
supervision [ˌsjuːpə'vɪʒən]　　*n.* 监督；管理

PART I EMERGENCY EQUIPMENT

Technical Terms

oral-nasal mask	口鼻面罩
self-contained breathing system	自主式呼吸系统
portable oxygen system	便携氧气系统
the oxygen tank	氧气瓶
relief valve	释放阀门

Notes

1. The portable oxygen system is a self-contained breathing system offering demand, pressure-demand and constant flow capabilities. 便携式氧气系统是一个独立的供氧系统，能够提供需氧量的需求，具有压力设定和流量恒定的功能。

2. It has two constant flow outlets, a relief valve protecting the low-pressure system from over-pressurization, a fingertip controlled ON-OFF valve, a pressure gauge indicating oxygen supply, a high-pressure safety relief device, a demand or pressure-demand regulator, a carrying strap, and a soft rubber-like oral-nasal mask with the flow indicator assembly.
   便携氧气瓶的基本组成部件包括：
   constant flow outlet 恒定流量供氧出口，
   pressure gauge indicating oxygen supply 氧气压力指示表，
   fingertip controlled on-off valve 阀门开关，
   pressure-demand regulator 压力设定调节开关，
   flow indicator assembly 流量指示器。

3. This equipment is intended to be used only for aviation applications and is to be used only by or under the supervision of a crew member trained and qualified. 这个设备适用于航空，并且只能在培训后有资格的机组人员的指导下使用。

Exercises

I. Please answer the following questions.

1. What are the main components of the portable oxygen cylinder in the cabin?
2. What should be paid attention to when using the portable oxygen cylinder in the cabin?
3. According to the context, what do you think of the procedures of the preflight check of this equipment?

II. Focusing on Practice

Objective:

Master the basic use of the portable oxygen cylinder in the cabin.

Suggestions:

Practice can be fullfilled through grouping in the class. All the process should be timed by the group leader or the instructor.

Section 8 Portable Breathing Equipment

Portable breathing equipment (smoke hoods with oxygen), PBE for short, is installed in the passenger cabin. The smoke hoods provide an oxygen supply and smoke protection and should be used when fighting a fire.

The portable devices consist of protective breathing equipment and portable high-pressure oxygen cylinders with continuous flow oxygen mask. The breathing hood is stored under a vacuum-sealed pouch, which is mounted inside a box. Two tamper-evident seals secure the pouch within the container and serve as tamper indicators. The smoke hood is based on a chemical air regeneration system, located in the breathing bag. An oronasal mask allows inhalation of regenerated air and returns the exhaled air to the regeneration system. The hood

PART I EMERGENCY EQUIPMENT

is serviceable, as long as the yellow indicator on the case is not broken and operates for at least 20 minutes.

The smoke hood is placed over the head and activated by a starter lanyard. The protective breathing equipment protects the user's eyes and respiratory system against heat, smoke, and/or noxious gases. It ensures that a minimum of 15 minutes of total autonomy is available. The PBE is readily available to cabin attendants. The primary purpose of the PBE is to supply oxygen to cabin attendants in the event of a fire, smoke and/or noxious gases. It enables them to move about freely in the cabin and extinguish a fire. It can also be used in the event of cabin depressurization.

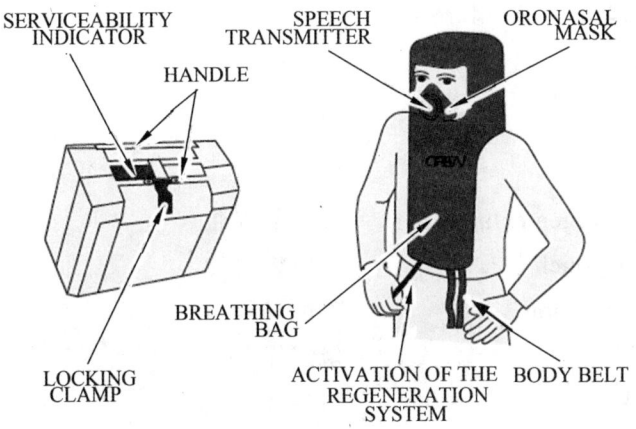

Figure 1.18

Words and Expressions

continuous [kənˈtɪnjuəs]   *adj.* 连续的；延伸的

vacuum [ˈvækjuəm]   *n.* 真空，空白

mount [maʊnt]   *vt.& vi.* 安装，架置；镶嵌，嵌入

tamper [ˈtæmpə]   *vt. & vi.* （用不正当手段）影响，干预

secure [sɪˈkjuə]   *vt. & vi.* 保护；获得安全，变得安全

pouch [paʊtʃ]   *n.* 小袋

regeneration [rɪˌdʒenəˈreɪʃən]　*n.* [生]再生；恢复
oronasal [ˌɔːrəʊˈneɪzəl]　*n.& adj.* 口鼻(的)
inhalation [ˌɪnhəˈleɪʃən]　*n.* 吸入；吸入剂，吸入物
exhale [eksˈheɪl]　*vt. & vi.* 发散出；放出
serviceable [ˈsɜːvɪsəbəl]　*adj.* 有用的，可供使用的；耐用的
activate [ˈæktɪveɪt]　*vt.* 使活动，起动，触发
lanyard [ˈlænjəd]　*n.* 系索
autonomy [ɔːˈtɒnəmɪ]　*n.* 自治，自治权；自主权
noxious [ˈnɒkʃəs]　*adj.* 有害的，有毒的
minimum [ˈmɪnɪməm]　*n.* 最低限度
　　　　　　　　　　　　adj. 最低的
as long as　只要，如果，既然

Technical Terms

smoke hood　　　　　　　　　　防烟面罩
high-pressure oxygen cylinder　　高压氧气瓶
vacuum-sealed pouch　　　　　　真空密封袋
cabin depressurization　　　　　　客舱释压
starter lanyard　　　　　　　　　触发绳
oronasal mask　　　　　　　　　口鼻面罩

Notes

1. Portable breathing equipment (smoke hoods with oxygen), PBE for short, is installed in the passenger cabin.
   Portable breathing equipment，PBE 防烟面罩，也有称为全脸式集成烟雾护目镜氧气面罩，是飞机上用于保护机组人员呼吸系统的应急设备之一。
   注：氧气系统是飞机上独立的一个系统，在本章后面的内容中，会完整地介绍其他的氧气设备。

2. The breathing hood is stored under a vacuum-sealed pouch, which is mounted inside a box. 由真空袋子包裹的防烟面罩储藏在一个盒子里。

3. The protective breathing equipment protects the user's eyes and respiratory system against heat, smoke, and/or noxious gases. 防烟面罩保护使用者的眼睛以及呼吸系统免受热气、烟雾和毒气的伤害。
4. It enables them to move about freely in the cabin and extinguish a fire. It can also be used in the event of cabin depressurization. 它可以让乘务员在灭火时，自由地行走于客舱内，在客舱释压的情况下也可以使用。

Exercises

Ⅰ. **Please answer the following questions.**

1. What is the PBE used for?
2. What should be paid attention to during the use of the PBE?

Ⅱ. **Discuss the cautions before and after using the PBE.**

Ⅲ. **Focusing on Practice**

Objective:
　　Learners should dress up the PBE tight and right within the time limitation. Keep in mind the precautions of using the PBE.

Suggestions:
　　No matter what type of PBE is used, practice can be fullfilled through grouping in the class. All the process should be timed by the group leaders or the instructors.

Section 9　Life Vest

　　Life vests are for emergency use, particularly for application in commercial passenger aircraft flying over water. It is presently common practice to equip commercial airliners with inflatable life vests for use by both crews and passengers in the event that the aircraft is forced down or "ditched" in water. Such inflatable life vests have heretofore been used, however, have been stowed under the seat. Generally the life vests are available in passenger yellow or crew molten orange.

There is a life vest for every crewmember–flight crew and cabin crew–on board the aircraft. The life vests for the flight crew are stowed in each cockpit seat and those for the cabin crew are stowed in each cabin attendant seat. There are life vests for all passengers as well. Additionally there may be installed some spare life vests in the cabin, some infant life vests, even baby survival raft.

The life vests have these main components: inflatable cells, waist belt harness with buckle and harness-pull-tab, gas inflation system, oral inflation system, water-activated light assembly and whistle.

Each life vest shows the instruction for its use. One should locate the life vest under the seat, grasp the poly bag and tear the pull-tab free of the bag, thus open the sewn end and unroll it. Hold the life vest on each side of the neck opening and put the head through the opening. Run the waist belt harness around the back of the waist and back to the front. Hold the buckle ends; pull the harness pull-tab to tighten snugly. It is necessary to note the danger of finger clamping by closing the buckle and make sure that the life vest is drawn firmly against the body.

Pulling the red "Jerk-To-Inflate" tabs can inflate the buoyancy chambers with the gas inflation system. With the oral inflator system you can inflate the life vest yourself by blowing into the end of the tubes by mouth. If more or less pressure in the life vest is necessary, use the oral inflator system. The oral inflation system in each inflatable cell can also be used to release gas by depressing the valves at the tube ends. Do not inflate the life vest inside the aircraft. An inflated life vest may hinder the person who wears it from leaving the aircraft through the emergency exit and may cause injury or death. Oral inflation prior to gas inflation will cause excessive pressure which may burst the life vest.

PART | *EMERGENCY EQUIPMENT*

The light assembly activates automatically when the battery is immersed in water.

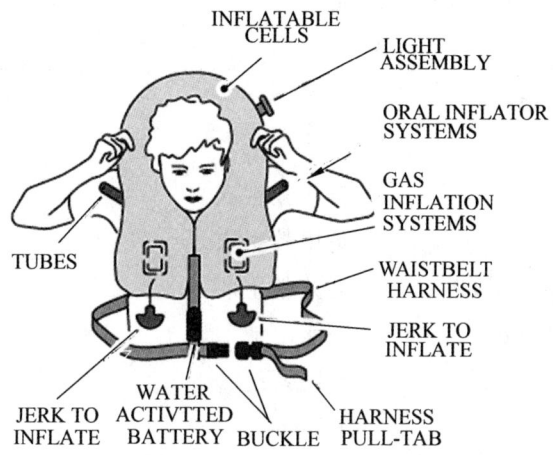

Figure 1.19

Words and Expressions

inflatable [ɪnˈfleɪtəbl]   *adj.* 可膨胀的，可充气的
                n. 可充气物品
ditch [dɪtʃ]   *vi.* 使（飞机）在海上紧急降落，（在海上）迫降
heretofore [ˈhɪətəˌfɔː, -ˌfəʊr]   *adv.* 在此以前
molten [ˈməʊltən]   *adj.* 熔化的，熔融的；铸造的
harness [ˈhɑːnɪs]   *n.* 马具，挽具；降落伞背带
buckle [ˈbʌkl]   *vt.& vi.* 用搭扣扣紧；（使）变形，弯曲
        n. 搭扣，扣环
poly [ˈpɒlɪ]   *abbr.* 聚乙烯（全称 polyethylene）
snugly [ˈsnʌglɪ]   *adv.* 紧贴地；贴身地；暖和舒适地；安适地
clamp [klæmp]   *vt.& vi.* 夹紧，夹住；锁住
hinder [ˈhɪndə]   *vt.& vi.* 阻碍，妨碍；成为阻碍
excessive [ɪkˈsesɪv]   *adj.* 过度的，极度的；过分的

burst [bə:st]　　*vi.* 爆裂，炸破；使爆炸

immerse [ɪˈmə:s]　　*vt.* 浸没；施浸礼；沉迷……中，陷入

prior to　在前，居先，比……在先

Technical Terms

infant life vest	婴儿救生衣
spare life vest	备用救生衣
baby survival raft	婴儿救生船
water activated battery	海水电池
light assembly	照明系统

Notes

1. It is presently common practice to equip commercial airliners with inflatable life vests for use by both crews and passengers in the event that the aircraft is forced down or "ditched" in water. 目前，航空公司都会给机组以及乘客配备救生衣以应对水上迫降情况的出现。

2. The life vests are available in passenger yellow or crew molten orange. 救生衣有两种颜色：一种是黄色的乘客救生衣，一种是橙黄色的机组救生衣。
   注：这两种颜色都是警告色，救援人员在茫茫大海中极易发现和区别。

3. The life vests have these main components: inflatable cells, waist belt harness with buckle and harness-pull-tab, gas inflation system, oral inflation system, water-activated light assembly and whistle. 救生衣上主要包括气囊、腰带、高压气瓶、人工充气管、海水电池和哨子。
   注：救生衣是用尼龙材料做成的高低两个气囊，起到了双安全的作用。亮片气囊中有左右各一的两个高压气瓶，只需分别拉动两边的红色把手，即可在 2 秒钟内充气。不同厂家的救生衣，腰带的设计结构会有所不同，但功能都是相同的。

PART Ⅰ *EMERGENCY EQUIPMENT*

4. It is necessary to note the danger of finger clamping by closing the buckle and make sure that the life vest is drawn firmly against the body. 特别要指出的是在使用搭扣时要小心手指被夹住，并且救生衣的穿戴一定要松紧合适。

5. Oral inflation prior to gas inflation will cause excessive pressure which may burst the life vest. 如果人工充气先于自动充气，救生衣会因过多的压力而破裂。

Exercises

Ⅰ. **Please answer the following questions.**

1. What's the difference of these two kinds of life vests?
2. What are the main components of life vests?
3. What types of life vest are installed on an aircraft?

Ⅱ. **Focusing on Practice**

<u>Objective</u>:

　　Learners should dress up the life vest tight and right within the time limitation.

　　Master the folding method of the life vest after using.

<u>Suggestions</u>:

　　Practice can be fullfilled through grouping in the class. All the process should be timed by the group leaders or the instructors.

Section 10　Life Raft

　　A life raft is a piece of safety equipment which is used to provide emergency transportation to get people away from a sinking. Life rafts are inflatable. They are made from durable materials. This design is intended to ensure that the raft inflates quickly in an emergency. In addition to providing a mode of transit, a life raft usually also provides shelter so that people are at least partially protected from the elements.

Several life rafts are stowed on board the aircraft in the overhead compartments in the front and aft cabin. Basically different aircrafts will be installed with different types of life rafts. Here is one of the life rafts.

The life raft herein is for 25 persons normal capacity, 38 persons overload capacity and has these main components:

–Sea anchor

–Boarding ladder

–Hook knife

–Life line

–Locator light

–Mooring line

–Inflation assembly.

Each life raft shows the instruction for its use. The life raft must be prepared for launching, including the survival kit attached. The lanyard line must be attached to a fixed part of the aircraft. Pull the inflation handle located in a pocket on the carrying case. This will initiate the inflation of the buoyancy chamber. Board the raft and cut the lanyard line.

There are a number of commercially produced pre-assembled aviation survival kits available. When ditching, remember to attach the kit to the raft or the slide ahead manually.

The basic list of contents for these survival kits doesn't vary a lot. A survival kit needs to supply or give you the tools to furnish medical care, shelter, signaling to attract rescue and sustenance in the emergency situation. It mainly contains the following items.

PART I   EMERGENCY EQUIPMENT

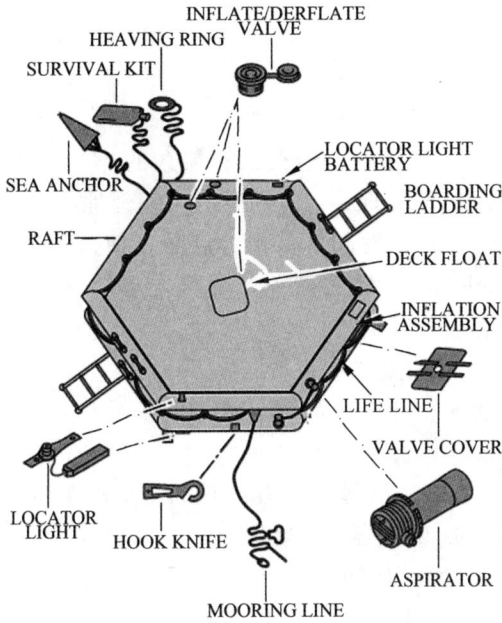

Figure 1.20

canopy	aspirin
oar	antiseptic swabs
pliers	ammonia inhalation
gloves	blister burn ointment
mooring line	dimenhydrinate
spare cord	flashlight
hand pump	safety whistle
utility knife	flare kit
dehydrated sponge	chemical light stick
bailing bucket	signal mirror
water punch	sea dye marker
repair kit	survival book
raft manual	shark chaser
compass and match	sea water desalting kit
first aid kit	fishing kit
water purification tablet	food
water germicidal tablet	

Words and Expressions

durable ['djuərəbl]　*adj.* 耐用的，耐久的；持久的
partially ['pɑ:ʃəli]　*adv.* 部分地；[古]偏袒地，偏爱地
initiate [ɪ'nɪʃɪeɪt]　*vt.* 开始，发起；传授，启蒙，使入门
sustenance ['sʌstənəns]　*n.* 食物，营养，养料
anchor ['æŋkə]　*n.* 锚
mooring ['muərɪŋ]　*n.* 停泊处
launch [lɔ:ntʃ]　*vt.* 发射；开展（活动、计划等）
　　　　　　　　vi. 投入；着手进行
heaving ['hi:vɪŋ]　*n.* 举起，拿起；扔去；升沉（运动）
aspirator ['æspɪreɪtə]　*n.* 吸气器；吸尘器
chamber ['tʃeɪmbə]　*n.* 室，房间
canopy ['kænəpi]　*n.* 任何悬于上空的覆盖物；天棚
bailing ['beɪlɪŋ]　*n.* （凿井时用吊桶）排水
sponge [spʌndʒ]　*n.* 海绵
cord [kɔ:d]　*n.* 绳子，索，弦，缆，带
plier ['plaɪə]　*n.* 钳子（如老虎钳、手钳、扁嘴钳等），镊子
desalt [di:'sɔ:lt]　*vt.* 除去……的盐分
compass ['kʌmpəs]　*n.* 罗盘，指南针
oar [ɔ:]　*n.* 桨，橹；划手
　　　　　vi. 划（行）
dye [daɪ]　*vt. & vi.* 给……上色；着色
lanyard ['lænjəd]　*n.* 安全绳
dehydrate [di:'haɪˌdreɪt]　*vt. & vi.* 使脱水，使干燥
adhesive [əd'hi:sɪv]　*n.* 黏合剂
　　　　　　　　　　adj. 可黏着的，黏性的
ammonia [ə'məʊnjə]　*n.* 氨，氨水
inhalation [ˌɪnhə'leɪʃən]　*n.* 吸入物，吸入药；吸入法
purification [ˌpjʊərəfɪ'keɪʃən]　*n.* 净化，提纯
antiseptic [ˌæntɪ'septɪk]　*adj.* 防腐的，杀菌的
　　　　　　　　　　　　n. 防腐剂

PART | *EMERGENCY EQUIPMENT*

antiemetic [ˌæntɪˈmetɪk] *adj.* 止呕吐的
                          n. 止吐药
ointment [ˈɔɪntmənt] *n.* 软膏，油膏
dimenhydrinate [ˌdaɪmenˈhaɪdrəˌneɪt] *n.* 乘晕宁

Technical Terms

overhead compartment	行李架
mooring line	连接绳
signal mirror	反光镜
dehydrated sponge	脱水海绵
chemical light stick	化学安全棒
utility knife	工具刀
ammonia inhalation	氨吸入剂
sea dye marker	海水着色剂

Notes

1. A life raft is a piece of safety equipment which is used to provide emergency transportation to get people away from a sinking. 救生船是在紧急情况下帮助人们摆脱溺水的一种设备。
   注：机上救生船除了有常见的圆形船以外，还包括其他形式的船体。船的大小和数量也根据飞机上座位数量的多少来配备。

2. In addition to providing a mode of transit, a life raft usually also provides shelter so that people are at least partially protected from the elements. 除了作为交通工具，救生船也能为乘客们提供遮风避雨的地方。

3. The life raft must be prepared for launching, including the survival kit attached.
   救生船要随时做好使用的准备，救命包也要和船体连接好。

4. When ditching, remember to attach the kit to the raft or the slide ahead manually.
   当水上迫降的时候，一定记得提前将救命包系在救生船上。

5. The basic list of contents for these survival kits doesn't vary a lot. 救命包里的物品基本都是大同小异的。

Exercises

Ⅰ. Please answer the following questions.

1. What are the main components of the life raft?
2. How do you operate a life raft according to the text?
3. What does the survival kit consist of?

Ⅱ. Focusing on Practice

Objective:

Master the basic operating method of the life raft in the cabin and in water.

Suggestions:

Practice can be fullfilled through grouping in the class. All the process should be timed by the group leaders or the instructors.

Section 11　Portable Emergency Equipment in the Cockpit

Flight Deck Escape Rope

Two Flight Deck Escape Ropes are on board the aircraft:

—one in a RH stowage above the RH sliding window on the side of the overhead panel, marked by a red label.

—one in LH stowage above the LH sliding window on the side of the overhead panel, marked by a red label.

The Flight Deck Escape Rope is 5.5 m (18 ft.) long and knotted. The rope is connected with one end to the structure of the aircraft. The rope and the attachment can support a load of 900 kg (1984 lb.).

PART | *EMERGENCY EQUIPMENT*

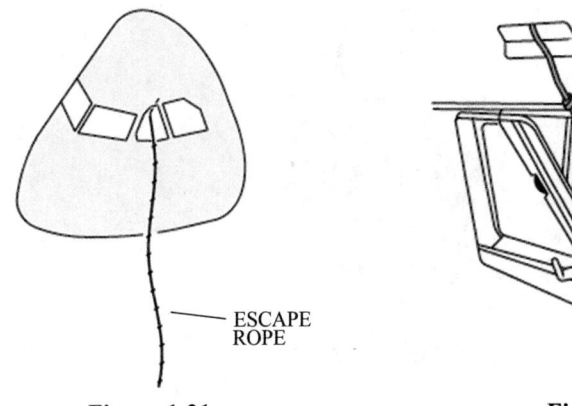

Figure 1.21   **Figure 1.22**

Crash Axe

The crash axes are used to cut through light structures, panels and windows. They have insulated handles which are resistant to high voltages. The crash axes are put into brackets on board in the cockpit of the aircraft.

Figure 1.23

Fire-fighting Gloves

Fire-fighting gloves are kept in pockets on board of the aircraft. The gloves are designed to provide limited protection against injuries to the hand during conventional firefighting. They are for use by crew member to grasp hot metal or burning parts. The gloves are resistant to tears and cuts and provide insulation for the skin.

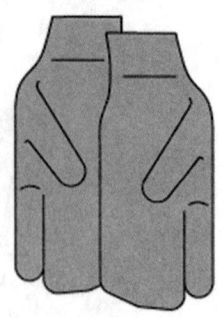

Figure 1.24

Words and Expressions

knot [nɒt]　　*n.* 结，绳结；[航]节（浬/小时），浬，海里
voltage ['vəʊltɪdʒ]　　*n.* 电压，伏特数
insulation [ˌɪnsə'leɪʃən, ˌɪnsjə-]　　*n.* 隔离，隔绝；绝缘；隔音
protection against　　对……的防护
be resistant to　　抵抗……的

Technical Terms

escape rope　　　　　　逃离绳
sliding window　　　　　推拉窗

Notes

1. The crash axes are put into brackets on board in the cockpit of the aircraft. 救生斧位于飞机的驾驶舱。在这里，除了在飞机的驾驶舱会有救生斧，机上的货舱通常也会配备。
2. The Flight Deck Escape Rope is 5.5 m (18 ft.) long and knotted. 驾驶舱逃离绳长约 5.5 米，每段都有打结。
驾驶舱逃离绳主要是在驾驶舱门无法正常使用的时候，帮助机组人员从窗户逃离的工具；在客舱，也配备了相应的绳索，辅助乘客从机翼安全撤离。

PART I EMERGENCY EQUIPMENT

Exercises

Please answer the following questions.

1. Where is the escape rope located?
2. What is the feature of the rope?
3. When can the crash axe be used and where is the crash axe installed?
4. Can the gloves be used by anyone on board? When can the fire-fighting gloves be used?

CHAPTER 2 FIXED EMERGENCY EQUIPMENT

Section 1 Emergency Locator Transmitter System (ELT System)

One ELT system is on board of the aircraft and has these components: emergency locator transmitter (ELT) unit with an aircraft identification module (AIM), remote control panel (RCP) and the antenna. The ELT unit and the AIM are installed in the AFT cabin area, above the RH ceiling panel in a support assembly. The ELT unit and AIM are permanently fixed to the aircraft. The RCP is installed in the cockpit area on the cockpit overhead panel. The antenna is installed on the upper external fuselage in the AFT aircraft area, just forward of the vertical stabilizer. The ELT beacon does not replace the survival ELT. The existence of the survival ELT is in addition necessary.

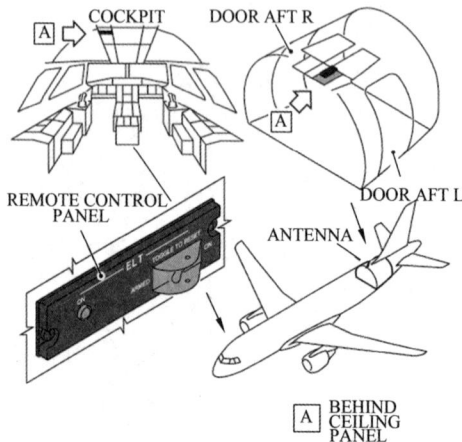

Figure 2.1

PART I EMERGENCY EQUIPMENT

The ELT System transmits on 3 frequencies, 121.5 MHz (civil) and 243 MHz (military) homing signals and with 406 MHz to the COSPAS-SARSAT satellite system. The components of the ELT system are–an integrated G-switch, an electronic assembly, a battery pack, interfaces for connecting to the aircraft structure, antenna, RCP and a switch. The RCP is an enclosed box with a lighted front panel, an ARM/ON switch, an ON indicator, a black panel with a connector to connect the RCP to ELT unit, and an identification placard. The antenna is connected by coaxial cable to the ELT unit.

The ELT system operates in these two configurations: automatically or manually.

The switch of the ELT unit is in the ARM position. In this configuration the unit is capable of detecting an activation signal from either the integrated G-switch or the RCP. Receiving an activation signal, the ELT unit switches to the transit mode and begins to transmit the signals. The ELT-system can be activated manually either from the RCP or from the transmitter unit. The toggle switch on the panel of the transmitter unit must be set to the ARMED position. The toggle switch on the RCP has to be set to the ON position.

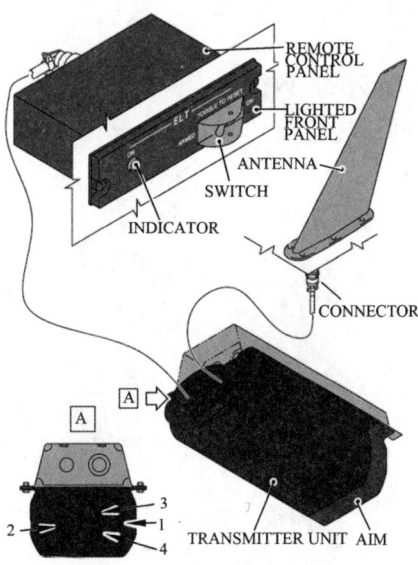

Figure 2.2

Words and Expressions

module ['mɒdju:l]　　n. 模件，组件，程序片，指令组
permanently ['pɜ:mənəntlɪ]　　adv. 永久地，不变地
external [eks'tɜ:nl]　　adj. 外面的，外部的
fuselage ['fju:zɪlɑ:ʒ]　　n. 机身
interface ['ɪntəfeɪs]　　n. 界面
　　　　　　　　　　vi. 连接
enclose [ɪn'kləʊz]　　vt. 把……围起来；把……装入信封，附入
fiberglass ['faɪbəglɑ:s]　　n. 玻璃纤维，玻璃丝
radome ['reɪdəʊm]　　n. 天线屏蔽器
aluminum [ə'lu:mənəm]　　n. 铝
alloy ['ælɔɪ]　　n. 合金
element ['elɪmənt]　　n. 成分，要素，原件
coaxial [kəʊ'æksəl]　　adj. 同心的；同轴的
configuration [kən,fɪgju'reɪʃən]　　n. 构造，形状，外貌，轮廓
switch [swɪtʃ]　　n. 开关
　　　　　　　　　vt. & vi. 转变，改变
switch to　切换到，转到，转变成
toggle ['tɒgl]　　n. 肘节

Technical Terms

COSPAS-SARSAT	全球卫星搜救系统
coaxial cable	同轴电缆
G-switch	惯性开关
RCP	遥控板；遥控台
toggle switch	肘节开关

PART I **EMERGENCY EQUIPMENT**

Notes

1. The ELT unit and the AIM are installed in the AFT cabin area, above the RH ceiling panel in a support assembly. 无线定位发报机和飞机识别模块安装在客舱的后部，右侧天花板上方。
注：前面学习过的便携式发报机是被安放在飞机上的指定位置，在撤离时带离飞机的；而这里的无线定位发报机是固定在飞机机体上，用于救援识别飞机的位置。
2. The ELT System transmits on 3 frequencies, 121.5 MHz (civil) and 243 MHz (military) homing signals and with 406 MHz to the COSPAS-SARSAT satellite system.
固定的发报机和便携式发报机所发射的频率是一致的。这三种频率也是国际通用的求救频率。
3. The ELT system operates in these two configurations: automatically or manually. 无线发报系统可以自动工作，也可以手动操作。

Exercises

Please answer the following questions.

1. What are the differences between ELT beacon and ELT system?
2. How many ways can be used in operation of the ELT?
3. What are the frequencies of the emergency signal?

Section 2 Doors and Exits in the Cabin

The aircraft has four cabin doors and four dedicated emergency exits. The second door (emergency exit) on the left hand side is used as a mid passenger door. Here are the Airbus aircraft doors and exits. The cabin doors have an initial opening movement to the inside, and then they open outwards. The emergency exits open inward and are located above the wing box. All doors are used as emergency exits in case of an emergency evacuation. All doors and exits are provided with an emergency evacuation facility. In cabin doors it is stowed in a container hinged on the lower part of the doors; in emergency exits it is stowed below the cabin floor.

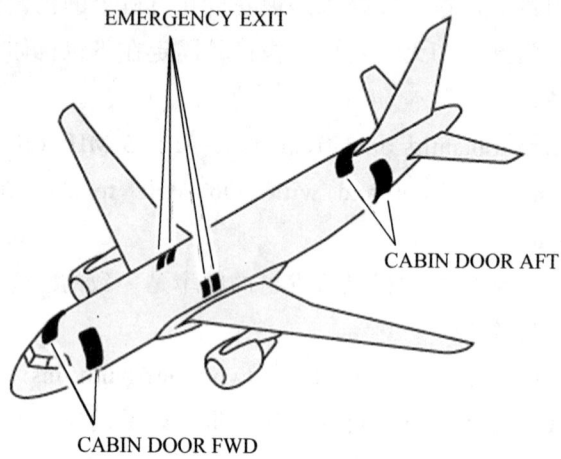

Figure 2.3　Location of Doors/Exits

Cabin Door

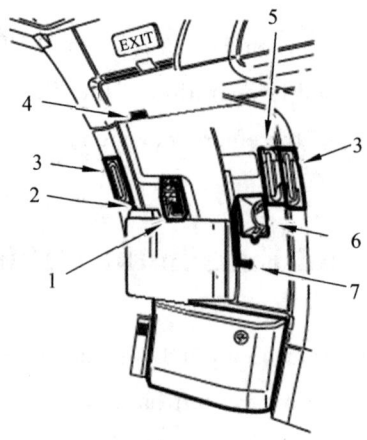

Figure 2.4

PART I EMERGENCY EQUIPMENT

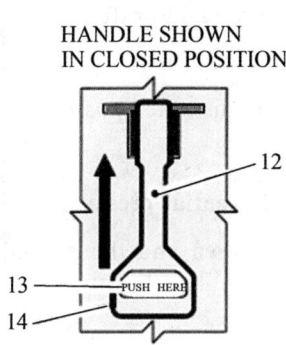

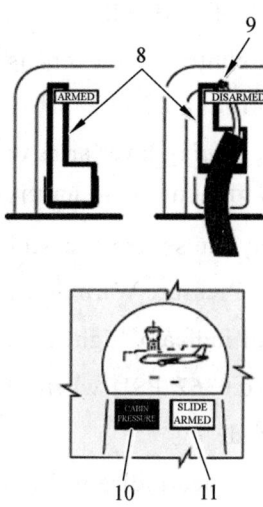

Figure 2.5   **Figure 2.6**

1 Arming System

It consists of the slide arming lever and a safety pin.

2 Gust Lock

A gust lock secures the door in its open position.

3 Assist Handles

Assist handles is used to hold onto when opening or closing the door.

4 Locking Indicator

A door locking indicator indicates the door status.

—The information UNLOCKED on a red background is given when the door is not in its closed/locked position.

—The information LOCKED on a green background is given when the door is fully closed and locked.

5 Door Assist Handle

An assist handle is used when opening or closing the door.

6 Observation Window

An observation window has two indicator lights visible from inside and outside.

7　Door Control Handle

A door control handle opens and closes the door from inside.

8　Slide Arming Lever

A slide arming lever arms or disarms the door slide/slide-raft.

9　Safety Pin with Warning Flag

A safety pin secures the slide arming lever in the disarmed position.

10　Cabin Pressure Warning Light

The red indicator light flashes if the cabin differential pressure is above 2.5 mbar (0.0362 PSI) when all engines are shut down and the related door is disarmed.

11　Door Armed Indicator Light

The white indicator light lights up steadily when the door is in ARMED mode and the door control handle is moved up.

12　Exterior Door Control Handle

It consists of a flap and a handle.

13　Flap

To release the exterior door control handle from its closed position.

14　Handle

A handle opens and closes the door from outside.

Besides the Airbus aircraft doors and exits, the Boeing aircraft has its own features. The basic airplane has six passenger entry doors, two emergency doors, one flight deck door (the flight deck/passenger cabin entry), and two cargo doors. It also has electrical equipment and forward equipment bay access doors. The flight deck has two windows, one on the left and one on the right, can be opened by the flight crew.

The passenger entry doors are used to enter and exit the airplane, and also serve as emergency exits. The passenger entry doors are paired along the airplane fuselage. The doors can be opened or closed manually from inside or outside of the airplane.

PART I EMERGENCY EQUIPMENT

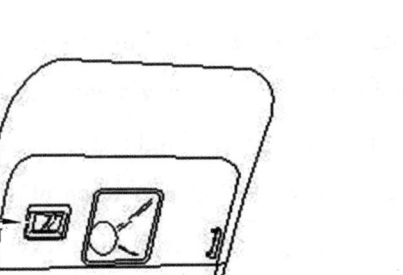

Figure 2.7

The entry doors are plug-type doors. During opening, the door first moves inward, then rotates outward and forward. Each door is held in the open position by a gust lock. The gust lock drops into a latch on the upper hinge arm as the door nears its forward limit of travel. Lifting the gust lock lever latches the gust lock lever in the UP position and releases the hinge arm, allowing the door to be closed. A window in each door allows observation outside of the airplane. An escape slide/raft is contained in a bustle on the lower inboard face of the door. A wide angle viewer is used for observing the outside of the airplane.

Operation of the Cabin Door

The cabin door can be operated from inside. If the red cabin pressure indicator flashes, do not force the handle to open the door. The slide arming lever must be in the DISARMED position and the safety pin must be installed. If cabin crew opens the door while the red cabin pressure indicator is flashing, there is a risk that the cabin door will open violently due to the cabin not being fully depressurized. The red indicator light flashes in case of a cabin differential pressure above 2.5 mbar (0.0362 psi) when all engines are shut down and the related door is disarmed. If the slide arming lever is not in the disarmed position the slide will be activated automatically by door opening. Then you should grasp one of the assist handles, lift the door control handle fully up and push the door outwards and then move it forward by using the assist handle until it locks in its fully open position. If closing door from inside, one should grasp the assist handle, press the gust lock simultaneously while pulling the support arm towards yourself. Move the door rearwards by using the assist handle. When the door is in front of its frame, pull the door inwards and lower the control handle. Finally, check whether the door is locked correctly: the door locking indicator must indicate LOCKED.

The cabin door can be operated from outside. Labels next to the exterior door control handle indicate how to operate the door from outside. One should look through the observation window and make sure that the RED cabin pressure indicator does not flash. Push the flap and grasp the handle, lift the handle fully up to the horizontal green line. Pull the door outwards and forward until it locks in its fully open position. When closing from outside, push the gust lock to unlock the door, move the door towards the frame, push it into the frame and lower the exterior door control handle.

When the emergency situation occurs, the door should open immediately with the slide. First, you must check whether the arming system is in ARMED mode, hold on to the assist handle and lift the door control handle rapidly fully up and release it. The door opens automatically and locks in its fully open position. If the pneumatic assistance of the door fails, push the door open manually.

PART I EMERGENCY EQUIPMENT

EMERGENCY EXIT

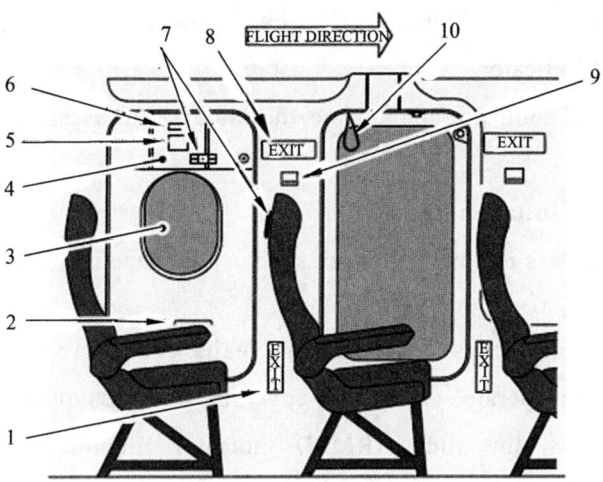

Figure 2.8 Controls and Indicators of the Emergency Exit

1 Exit Marker

In an emergency the EXIT markers situated on both sides of the emergency exit hatch are illuminated.

2 Handle Recess

The handle recess and the cover flap recess are used to remove the hatch.

3 Window

A normal window with a shade is integrated into the emergency exit hatch.

4 Handle Cover

The handle cover covers the hatch handle.

5 Hatch Handle (optional under Transparent Handle Flap)

An illuminated hatch handle to open and close the hatch from inside covered with a transparent handle flap.

6 Cover Flap Recess

The cover flap recess and the handle recess are used to remove the hatch.

7 Opening Instructions

You can find the opening instructions on the backs of the seats next to the emergency exits and on the hatch itself.

8 Exit Sign

The EXIT sign is illuminated in case of an emergency.

9 Slide Armed Indicator

A slide armed indicator to indicate the slide status is situated next to the hatch.

10 Slide Manual Inflation Handle

When the hatch is removed, you can see the slide manual inflation handle.

The emergency exits are over-wing exits. They are always in armed configuration. To operate, the handle cover must be removed by opening the cover flap recess, the slide ARMED indicator illuminates. If there is a transparent handle flap installed, lift it. Then pull down the hatch handle, it moves inwards. To inflate the escape slide, pull the slide manual inflation handle. The outside conditions must be checked before lifting up the door control handle.

Arming System

The arming system lever of a cabin door connects the girt bar, to which the escape slide is attached, to the cabin door (disarmed position) or to the cabin floor (armed position).

When the slide arming lever is in the DISARMED position, a safety pin with a red warning flag must be installed in order to indicate that the door is DISARMED and to prevent inadvertent movement of the slide arming lever.

In order to arm the door, the safety pin has to be removed and stowed in the hole provided on the door support arm for that purpose. Then the slide arming lever must be moved to the armed position. The door is now ready for flight.

When the slide arming lever is in the armed position, a flap moves over the disarmed safety pin hole which avoids the reinstalling of the safety pin. If the slide arming lever is in the armed position and the door is opened from outside, the lever will move automatically and mechanically to the disarmed position.

PART | *EMERGENCY EQUIPMENT*

Words and Expressions

dedicate ['dedɪkeɪt]　　*vt.* 奉献，献身
initial [ɪ'nɪʃəl]　　*adj.* 最初的；开始的；首字母的
outwards ['aʊtwədz, 'aʊtwərdz]　　*adv.* 向外地；外表地
inward ['ɪnwəd]　　*adj.* 向内的；内部的；本质上的
　　　　　　　　　　adv. 向内；内心里
evacuation [ɪˌvækju:'eɪʃən]　　*n.* 撤空；撤离；撤退；疏散
hinge [hɪndʒ]　　*n.* 铰链；枢要，中枢
　　　　　　　　vt. & vi. 用铰链连接；依……为转移
gust [gʌst]　　*n.* 一阵狂风；风味；突发的一阵
indicator ['ɪndɪˌkeɪtə]　　*n.* 指示器；[化]指示剂；指示者
rotate [rəʊ'teɪt]　　*vt. & vi.*（使某物）旋转；使转动；使轮流，轮换
fuselage ['fju:zɪlɑ:ʒ]　　*n.* [空]（飞机的）机身；火箭的外壳；弹体
pneumatic [nu:'mætɪk, nju:-]　　*adj.* 充气的；气动的；装满空气的
situate ['sɪtʃu:ˌeɪt]　　*vt.* 使位于，使处于……地位（位置）
illuminate [ɪ'lju:mɪneɪt]　　*vt. & vi.* 照亮，照明；阐明，说明
hatch [hætʃ]　　*n.*（船甲板或飞机底部装货物的）舱口；开口
transparent [træn'spærənt]　　*adj.* 透明的；含义清楚的，显而易见的
resistance [rɪ'zɪstəns]　　*n.* 抵抗；阻力；抗力；电阻
girt [gɜ:t]　　*v.* 束缚（gird 的过去式和过去分词）
inadvertent [ˌɪnəd'vɜ:tnt]　　*adj.* 不经意的，出于无心的；疏忽的，漫不经心的
reinstall [ˌri:ɪn'stɔ:l]　　*vt.* 使重新正式就职，重新设置
mechanically [mɪ'kænɪkəlɪ]　　*adv.* 机械方面地；机械地；物理上地

Technical Terms

emergency exit	应急出口
emergency evacuation	紧急撤离
arming system	预位系统
girt bar	滑梯杆
slide arming lever	滑梯预位手柄

Notes

1. The cabin doors have an initial opening movement to the inside, and then they open outwards. 舱门打开时，先朝内再朝外打开。

2. In cabin doors they are stowed in a container hinged on the lower part of the doors, in emergency exits they are stowed below the cabin floor. （滑梯）储藏在舱门的下部和紧急出口的下方。
注：舱门的位置不同，机型不同，滑梯的位置也会不同。

3. The red indicator light flashes if the cabin differential pressure is above 2.5 mbar (0.0362 PSI) when all engines are shut down and the related door is disarmed. 当所有的发动机停止工作，相应的舱门也处于解除预位状态，如果舱内压力超过 2.5 mbar (0.0362 psi)，红色的指示灯就会闪烁。

4. The gust lock drops into a latch on the upper hinge arm as the door nears its forward limit of travel. 当舱门前端到达尽头，扶手上的阵风锁锁住。

5. The emergency exits are over-wing exits. They are always in armed configuration. 紧急出口就是翼上出口，滑梯一直处于预位状态。

6. The arming system lever of a cabin door connects the girt bar, to which the escape slide is attached, to the cabin door (disarmed position) or to the cabin floor (armed position). 舱门预位手柄连接着滑梯杆，滑梯杆也连接着滑梯包。滑梯杆在解除预位的状态下连接着舱门，在预位状态下连接着舱门地板。

Exercises

Ⅰ. Please answer the following questions.

1. How do you operate the cabin door from inside and outside?
2. How do you operate the emergency exit?
3. What should you do before lift up the door control handle?
4. Are the emergency exits always in armed configuration?
5. If the slide arming lever is in the armed position and the door is opened from outside, what will happen then?

PART Ⅰ EMERGENCY EQUIPMENT

Ⅱ. Focusing on Practice

Objective:

Master the basic operation of the cabin doors.

Master the basic operation of the emergency exits.

Suggestions:

Practice can be fullfilled through grouping in the class. All the process should be timed by the group leader or the instructor.

Section 3 Slide Rafts

Slide rafts and escape slides are installed at each door/exit—a slide raft at each FWD and AFT cabin door and an escape slide at each pair of the over-wing emergency exits. They take care of a quick passenger and crew evacuation in case of an emergency. All slide rafts are of the dual lane type and function as an escape slide as well as an inflatable raft after ditching.

DOOR AND OVER-WING SLIDE LOCATION

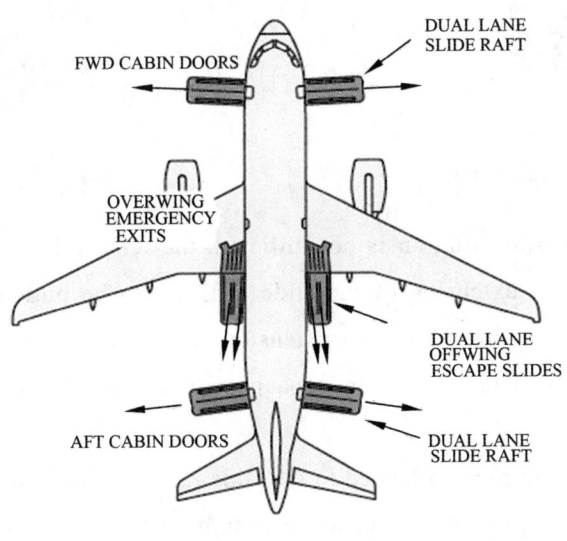

Figure 2.9

The deployment and inflation of the slide raft is automatically initiated when the door is opened in the ARMED mode. As the door opens, the girt tension pulls the pack board from the door. It falls below the doorsill, the speed lacing releases and the slide raft falls from the pack board. A firing lanyard actuates the regulator valve, primary gas is supplied to the aspirators and the inflation is initiated. An intermediated tie device restrains the slide raft to approximately one third of its extended length, to prevent that the slide raft inflates underneath the fuselage. When the slide raft becomes sufficiently pressurized, the intermediate tie releases and the slide raft extends outwards and downwards to contact the ground. The inflation reservoir sensors are connected to the CIDS and the pressure of the inflation cylinder is indicated on the FAP.

RELEASED SLIDERAFT

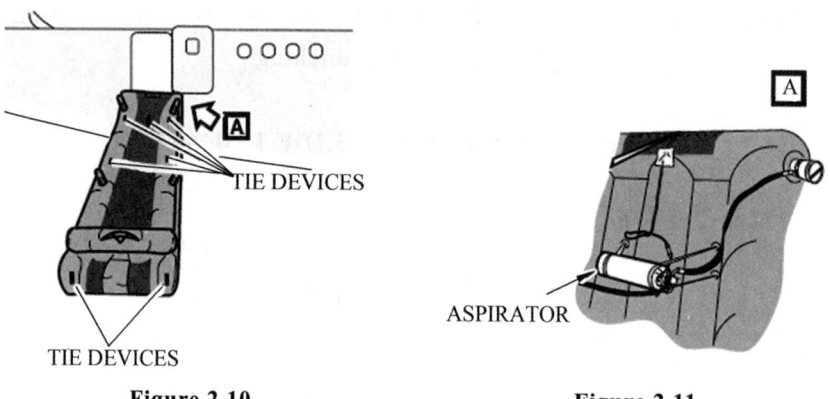

Figure 2.10   Figure 2.11

If the automatic inflation is not initiated, the red manual inflation handle, located on the girt extension of the slide raft, has to be pulled. The handle is located on the right side of the girt extension. The slide rafts inflate and deploy within 3 seconds. The evacuation capacity for one slide raft is 60 PAX per minute and lane.

There is a hand pump attached to the slide raft. The hand pump's function is to add air to either top chamber or lower chamber of the slide raft. The pump air

PART I EMERGENCY EQUIPMENT

fittings are clearly marked. There is also a canopy, which has a highly visible orange/yellow color. It gives the occupants protection against different environmental conditions.

After inflation, one of the crew members enters the slide raft and moves to the toe end. Then the passengers board the raft and start seating at the toe end. Last person to board the raft must be also a crew member who has to release the slide raft from the aircraft. To disconnect the raft from the aircraft, pull the disconnect handle. The slide raft is moored to the aircraft by means of a mooring line which is attached to the girt extension remaining on the cabin floor. To release the mooring line, pull the manual release handle located in a pouch on the top of the raft. If the mooring line is not released, use the hook knife for manual releasing.

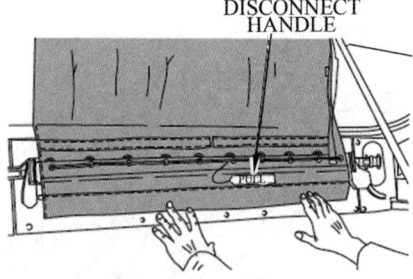

Figure 2.12

As mentioned before, a survival kit is provided for each slide raft. They are stowed in an overhead rack next to the FWD and AFT passenger doors, two in each. Attach one kit at each slide raft by means of a strap with snap hook.

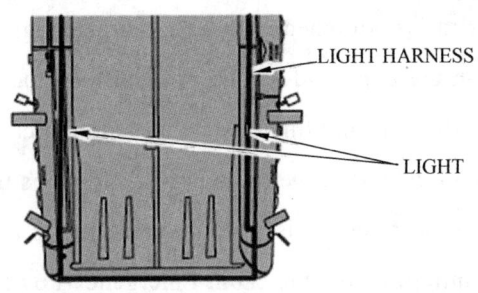

Figure 2.13

Only after ditching, if it happens that one cabin door is inoperative, its corresponding slide raft can be disconnected, transported and operated from any other cabin door, which has already been operated and its slide raft disconnected.

The off-wing slides are of dual lane type and are installed in the wing fuselage facing AFT of the over-wing exits. The slide inflation is automatically initiated if one emergency exit is opened. The escape slide inflates and deploys over the wing. The slide can also be inflated manually after the emergency exit is opened by pulling the manual inflation handle. It takes about 5 seconds for the escape slide to be ready for evacuation. If the slide automatic inflation does not occur, pull the manual inflation handle installed in the hatch frame of each emergency exit.

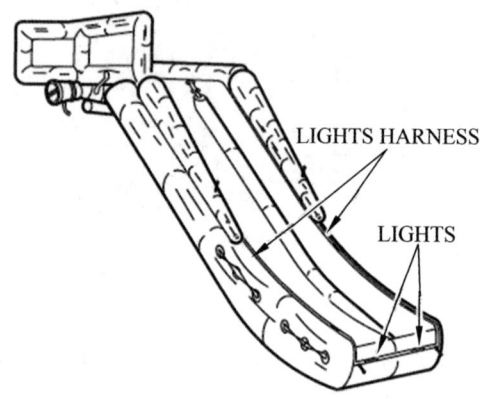

Figure 2.14

Each off-wing slide is equipped with an integrated lighting system. A light harness is attached on the upper side along of each longitudinal tube and across the bottom of the slide. The lighting system is automatically activated by the slide deployment. The lights have the same power supply as the cabin emergency lights. If no aircraft power supply is available, the lights are illuminated for a period of at least 10 minutes from the cabin Emergency Power Supply Units.

PART | EMERGENCY EQUIPMENT

Words and Expressions

lane [leɪn]　　*n.* 小路，小巷；航道，空中走廊
tension ['tenʃən]　　*n.* 紧张，不安；[物]张力，拉力
　　　　　　　　　　vt. 张紧；使紧张
doorsill ['dɔ:sɪl]　　*n.* 门槛
firing ['faɪərɪŋ]　　*n.* 开火
　　　　　　　　　　v. 开火，射击
actuate ['æktʃueɪt]　　*vt.* 使动作；开动
aspirator ['æspɪreɪtə]　　*n.* 吸液器，吸出器
intermediate [ˌɪntə'mi:diət]　　*adj.* 中间的，中级的
　　　　　　　　　　vi. 调解；干涉
restrain [rɪs'treɪn]　　*vt.* 抑制，压抑；限定，限制；制止；监禁
reservoir ['rezəvwɑ:]　　*n.* 蓄水池；贮液器；储藏；蓄积
sensor ['sensə, -ˌsɔ:]　　*n.* 传感器，灵敏元件
moor [muə]　　*vt.& vi.* 使停泊；系住；(把飞船)拴在系留塔上；固定
rack [ræk]　　*n.* 行李架；支架
canopy ['kænəpi]　　*n.* 天篷，华盖
occupant ['ɔkjəpənt]　　*n.* 占有人；居住者
inoperative [ɪn'ɒpərətɪv]　　*adj.* 不起作用的，无效的
corresponding [ˌkɒrɪs'pɒndɪŋ]　　*adj.* 相当的，对应的
integrated ['ɪntɪgreɪtɪd]　　*adj.* 完整的；整体的
longitudinal [lɒndʒɪ'tju:dɪnl]　　*adj.* 经度的；纵向的

Technical Terms

mooring line　　　　　　　　连接绳
snap hook　　　　　　　　　安全钩
CIDS　　　　　　　　　　　 客舱交互式数据系统
FAP　　　　　　　　　　　　前乘务员面板
Emergency Power Supply Units　　紧急供电系统

Notes

1. A firing lanyard actuates the regulator valve, primary gas is supplied to the aspirators and the inflation is initiated. 触发绳会打开调节阀门，气体被吸出器接收后，充气开始。

2. All slide rafts are of the dual lane type and function as an escape slide as well as an inflatable raft after ditching 所以的滑梯都是双通道，在水上迫降后同样可以作为救生船使用。

3. When the slide raft becomes sufficiently pressurized, the intermediate tie releases and the slide raft extends outwards and downwards to contact the ground. 当滑梯完全充气后，连接带释放开，滑梯朝外朝下伸展开，直到和地面接触到。

4. Only after ditching, if it happens that one cabin door is inoperative, its corresponding slide raft can be disconnected, transported and operated from any other cabin door, which has already been operated and its slide raft disconnected. 在水上迫降以后，如果出现了舱门不可用，相应的滑梯不能脱离飞机，那就从其他可用的舱门和滑梯离开。

5. If the slide automatic inflation does not occur, pull the manual inflation handle installed in the hatch frame of each emergency exit. 如果滑梯不能自动充气，拉动紧急出口门框内的人工充气手柄。

6. If no aircraft power supply is available, the lights are illuminated for a period of at least 10 minutes from the cabin Emergency Power Supply Units. 如果飞机的电源失效,滑梯的照明可以在紧急供电系统的支持下持续10分钟以上。

Exercises

Ⅰ. Please answer the following questions.

1. How do you operate the slide raft?
2. How do you operate the off-wing slides?
3. What should be done to disconnect the raft from the aircraft?
4. Is there any solution if the raft cannot be inflated automatically?

PART | *EMERGENCY EQUIPMENT*

II. Focusing on Practice

Objective:

Master the basic operation of the slide raft under different situations.

Suggestions:

Practice can be fullfilled through grouping in the class. All the process should be timed by the group leader or the instructor.

Section 4   Life Lines

Four additional life lines are provided. Only in the event of ditching, the life lines must be installed to assure the passengers a safe way to the ramp section.

The life lines are stowed in the hatrack above the RH and LH emergency exit doors. They must be fixed with the snap hook between the door-stop fitting located on the upper corner of the over-wing emergency exit door frames and the hook located on the center of the wing surface. After mooring, the life line must be pulled tight with the pull tab. The sliding buckle holds the life line tight for the correct length.

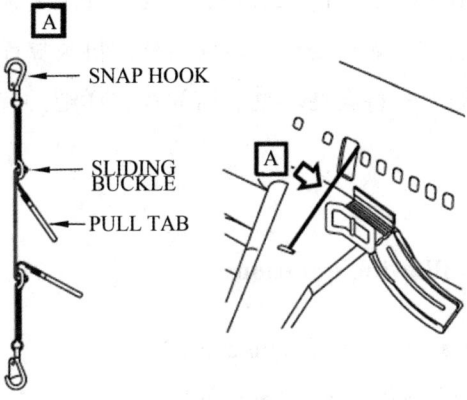

Figure 2.15

Words and Expressions

ramp [ræmp]   *n.* 斜道；（装车或上下飞机的）活动梯

ditch [dɪtʃ]   *n.*（在海上）迫降

hatrack [ˈhætræk]   *n.* 帽架

doorstop [ˈdɔːstɒp]   *n.* 制止门过开之物（如钩环）

buckle [ˈbʌkl]   *vt. & vi.* 用搭扣扣紧

　　　　　　　n. 搭扣，扣环

Technical Terms

snap hook　　　　　　　　安全挂钩

over-wing emergency exit　　翼上紧急出口

life line　　　　　　　　　　救生绳

Notes

Only in the event of ditching the life lines must be installed, to assure the passengers a safe way to the ramp section. 只要出现水上迫降，救生绳必须和飞机连接好，确保机上的乘客安全撤离到舱外的机翼翼面。

注：这种水上撤离的方式将会在本书后面的章节详细讲解到。

Exercises

Please answer the following questions.

1. How many life lines can be found on board?
2. What's the difference between a mooring line and a life line?

PART I EMERGENCY EQUIPMENT

Section 5   Passenger Emergency Oxygen System

Aircraft emergency oxygen systems are emergency equipment fitted to pressurized commercial aircraft, intended for use when the cabin pressurisation system has failed and the cabin altitude has climbed above a safe level. It consists of a number of individual oxygen masks stored in compartments above passenger seats, and some form of central oxygen generator. The passenger oxygen system is supplied by individual chemical oxygen generators. The oxygen system provides oxygen to the passenger, attendant stations and lavatory service units. The passenger oxygen masks and chemical oxygen generators are located above the passenger seats in Passenger Service Units (PSUs). An oxygen mask consists of a yellow, soft, silicone facial cup with white elastic bands for securing the mask to the passenger's face. This band is adjustable by pulling two ends looped through the facial cup. When the mask is pulled to the face, the firing pin is released and strikes the primer. This starts the ignition process inside the generator. Ten seconds later oxygen flows to each mask connected to that particular generator. The mask may also have a concentrator or re-breather bag that may or may not inflate depending on the cabin altitude, which has (in some instances) made passengers nervous that the mask was not providing adequate oxygen, causing some to remove them, who thereby suffer from hypoxia. The bag is attached to a tube, connected to the oxygen source in the compartment, allowing it to drop down and hang in front of the passengers.

Figure 2.16

Oxygen flows from a PSU generator when any mask hanging from that PSU is pulled sharply. Passenger oxygen masks can not deliver enough oxygen for sustained periods at high altitudes. This is why the flight crew needs to place the aircraft in a controlled emergency descent to a lower altitude where it is possible to breathe without emergency oxygen. Oxygen production cannot be shut off once a mask is pulled, and oxygen production typically lasts at least 15 minutes. During the production of oxygen, the generator becomes extremely hot and should not be touched. A burning smell may be noted and cause alarm among passengers, but this smell is a normal part of the chemical reaction. While the masks are being used, passengers are not allowed to leave their seat for any reason until it is safe to breathe without the emergency oxygen. If there is a fire on board the aircraft, masks are not deployed as the production of oxygen may further fuel the fire.

On most pressurized aircraft, if the cabin altitude reaches 14,000 feet, compartments containing the oxygen masks will open automatically, and the oxygen masks will drop down in front of the passenger. Oxygen masks may also drop on extremely rough landings or during severe turbulence if the oxygen mask panel becomes loose. Rows of seats typically have an extra mask in case someone has an infant in their lap, or someone in the aisle needs to grab one. Aircraft safety cards and in-flight safety demonstrations shown at the beginning of each flight explain the location and use of oxygen masks.

The cockpits of aircraft generally contain a separate oxygen system for the flight crew, and effective use of these has no doubt saved many aircraft. Hypoxia, which can cause severe disorientation and unconsciousness, sets in quickly; if a flight crew does not realize the cabin has decompressed, or is too slow to respond, they can quickly lose control of the aircraft.

PART | EMERGENCY EQUIPMENT

Words and Expressions

fit [fɪt]   *vt.& vi.*（使）适合；安装；合身
compartment [kəm'pɑ:tmənt]   *n.* 隔间（尤指火车车厢中的）；区划
silicone ['sɪlɪˌkəʊn]   *n.* 硅胶
elastic [ɪ'læstɪk]   *n.* 松紧带，橡皮圈
facial ['feɪʃəl]   *adj.* 面部的；面部用的
primer ['prɪmə]   *n.* 底漆；打底剂；火帽；雷管
concentrator ['kɒnsentreɪtə]   *n.* 集中器
re-breather [ri:'bri:ðə]   *n.* 换气器（由气体供给器和面罩组成的封闭环路式供氧系统）
hypoxia [haɪ'pɒksɪə]   *n.* 组织缺氧，氧不足
infant ['ɪnfənt]   *n.* 婴儿，幼儿
lap [læp]   *n.* 膝；下摆；一圈跑道；范围
disorientation [dɪsˌɔ:rɪən'teɪʃən]   *n.* 方向障碍，迷惑
unconsciousness [ʌn'kɒnʃəsnɪs]   *n.* 无意识；失去知觉

Technical Terms

passenger oxygen system   乘客氧气系统
cabin pressurisation system   客舱压力系统
chemical oxygen generator   化学氧气发生器
cabin altitude   座舱高度
rough landing   重着陆
in-flight safety demonstration   机上安全演示

Notes

1. Aircraft emergency oxygen systems are emergency equipment fitted to

pressurized commercial aircraft, intended for use when the cabin pressurisation system has failed and the cabin altitude has climbed above a safe level. 飞机紧急供氧系统是安装在增压后的航线运输机上的应急设备，用来应对客舱增压失效或者飞机爬升超过安全高度的情况。

2. The passenger oxygen masks and chemical oxygen generators are located above the passenger seats in Passenger Service Units (PSUs). 乘客氧气面罩和化学氧气发生器位于乘客座椅上方的乘客服务面板上。

3. The mask may also have a concentrator or re-breather bag that may or may not inflate depending on the cabin altitude, which has (in some instances) made passengers nervous that the mask was not providing adequate oxygen, causing some to remove them, who thereby suffer from hypoxia.

   面罩可能会附带一个集中器或者换气袋，它会根据座舱高度充气或不充气，这在某些情况下，会让乘客感觉到紧张，认为氧气面罩没有供养，导致乘客摘下面罩，面临缺氧危险。

4. Oxygen flows from a PSU generator when any mask hanging from that PSU is pulled sharply. 只要在掉落下来的面罩中有一个被拉动，氧气就自动开始流出。

5. If there is a fire on board the aircraft, masks are not deployed, as the production of oxygen may further fuel the fire. 如果机上着火了，氧气面罩是不会脱落的，因为这会加重火势。

Exercises

Ⅰ. Please answer the following questions.

1. What are the main components of the passenger emergency oxygen system?
2. When does the oxygen mask deploy?
3. How many ways can be applied to initiate the oxygen mask system?
4. According to your understanding, what should be paid attention to when using the mask?

PART I *EMERGENCY EQUIPMENT*

II. Focusing on Practice

The using of oxygen mask can be trained in two ways:
1. safety demonstraion
2. decompression procedures

Practice can be fullfilled through grouping in the class. All the process should be timed by the group leader or the instructor.

Section 6 Lavatory Fire Extinguish System

The modern aircraft lavatories' safety features include smoke detectors, waste receptacle, and portable fire containment Halon extinguishing bottles. These protective devices have been incorporated into aircraft lavatory designs due to fires that have started when the careless cigarette smoker of the past or the clandestine cigarette smoker of the present has incorrectly disposed of their smoking material.

Smoke Detector Assembly

Modern aircraft has smoke detector systems in the cargo holds, main avionics bay and passenger lavatories.

An ambient smoke detector is installed on each lavatory, located in the ceiling panel, beside the air extraction duct. The lavatory smoke detectors are interconnected to each other. They are part of a loop, containing the cargo smoke detectors (if installed), which is connected to the smoke detection control unit(SDCU). The SDCU sends the lavatory smoke warning signals to the ECAM and cabin intercommunication data system(CIDS).

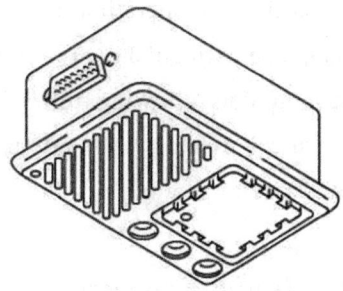

Figure 2.17

For lavatory fire extinguishing, a cabin portable fire extinguisher must be used.

Automatic Fire Extinguisher

The automatic fire extinguisher vessel contains extinguishing agent Halon 1211 (BCF). The extinguisher is designed to be installed within aircraft toilet cabinets in a fixed position and has the ability to detect and suppress fires. Each extinguisher consists of a spherical container on which pre-formed arms and mounting brackets are mounted. Each arm terminates in a special detector/discharge nozzle, which will discharge the extinguisher contents when a predetermined temperature is reached.

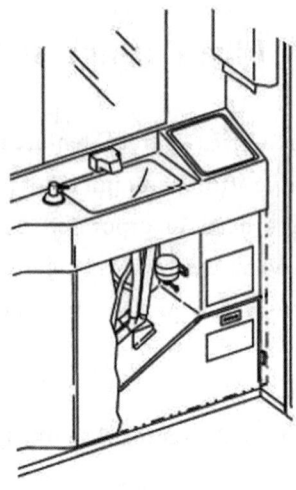

Figure 2.18

Once this temperature is reached, the extinguisher enters the active mode. On sensing the operation temperature, the heat sensitive capsule at the discharge end of the extinguisher arm/arms, melts around its periphery and is ejected from the arm thus allowing full discharge of the extinguishant. In discharge, the pressure indicator (if fitted) will fall to zero, likewise the pressure switch (if fitted) will operate.

Words and Expressions

receptacle [rɪˈseptəkəl]　　*n.* 容器，放置物品的地方

containment [kən'teɪnmənt]   n. 牵制；包含；容量；密闭度
incorporate [ɪn'kɔ:pəreɪt]   vt. & vi. 包含；吸收；合并；混合
be incorporated into   纳入
clandestine [klæn'destɪn]   adj. 秘密的；私下的；暗中的
dispose [dɪs'pəʊz]   vt. & vi. 处理，处置；安排
avionics [ˌeɪvi'ɒnɪks]   n. 航空电子设备，航空电子技术
extraction [ɪk'strækʃən]   n. 取出，抽出
duct [dʌkt]   n. 管，（电线，电缆等的）管道
          vt. 用导管输送；用管道供应
interconnect [ˌɪntəkə'nekt]   vt. & vi. （使）互相连接，互相联系
loop [lu:p]   n. 圈，环；回路
          vt.& vi. （使）成环；以环连结
vessel ['vesəl]   n. 容器；船，飞船；血管，管束
suppress [sə'pres]   vt. 镇压，压制；止住，忍住
spherical ['sfɪərɪkəl, 'sfer-]   adj. 球形的，球面的；天体的
terminate ['tə:mɪneɪt]   vt. & vi. 结束；使终结；到达终点站
          adj. 结束的
predetermine [ˌpri:dɪ'tɜ:mɪn]   vt. & vi. 预先裁定；注定
capsule ['kæpsju:l]   n. 胶囊；航天舱；小容器
periphery [pə'rɪfəri]   n. 边缘；圆周；外围；边缘地带

Technical Terms

cargo hold	货舱
avionics bay	电子舱
air extraction duct	气源选择导管
smoke detection control unit	烟雾探测控制组件
ECAM (electronic centralized aircraft monitoring)	飞机电子集中监控
cabin intercommunication data system	客舱内部通信数据系统

Notes

1. These protective devices have been incorporated into aircraft lavatory designs due to fires that have started when the careless cigarette smoker of the past or the clandestine cigarette smoker of the present has incorrectly disposed of their smoking material. 这些设备被安装在飞机的卫生间是因为抽完烟的粗心乘客或者偷偷正抽着烟的乘客会将未灭的烟头扔进垃圾箱，引起火灾。

2. Modern aircraft has smoke detector systems in the cargo holds, main avionics bay and passenger lavatories. 现代的飞机在货舱、电子舱和卫生间都装有烟雾探测系统。

3. They are part of a loop, containing the cargo smoke detectors (if installed), which is connected to the smoke detection control unit (SDCU). 它们是闭环的一部分，包括和烟雾探测控制组件连接的货舱烟雾探测器（如有安装）。

4. On sensing the operation temperature, the heat sensitive capsule at the discharge end of the extinguisher arm/arms, melts around its periphery and is ejected from the arm thus allowing full discharge of the extinguishant. 一旦探测到特定的温度，灭火器上的温度探头的边缘就会开始融化，灭火剂便喷射出来。

Exercises

Ⅰ. **Please answer the following questions.**

1. What does the lavatory fire extinguish system consist of?
2. How does the smoke detector function?
3. Discuss the difference of portable fire extinguisher and the automatic fire extinguisher.

Ⅱ. Focusing on Practice

Training section can be found in the fire entinguish procedure of this book. It can be fullfilled through grouping in the class. All the process should be timed by the group leader or the instructor.

Section 7 Emergency Lighting System

The passenger cabin interior and exterior lights are powered by the emergency lighting system. These lights provide illumination for evacuating the airplane. Emergency lighting is controlled by the Emergency Lights Switch on the overhead panel. The switch can be used to manually activate or arm the system for automatic operation.

All aircrafts have emergency lighting inside the cabin, along the aisles and over the exits. The aisle path lighting is alternating red and white lights on the floor, and on newer aircraft they can be on the outside of the aisle seats. The red lights indicate where the exits are. These are installed in case the cabin is dark and/or smoky so if you are down low to get out of the rising smoke, you can figure out where to exit. These lights, as well as the exit lights, will illuminate automatically if there is a disruption in the regular aircraft electrical power. These lights are connected to the hot battery bus.

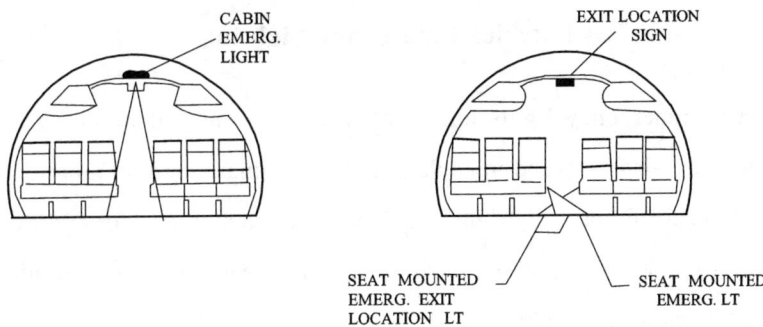

Figure 2.19

Interior Emergency Lighting

Interior Emergency Lighting consists of door, aisle, escape path, exit lights and luminescent exit signs. Escape Path Lighting consists of floor / seat mounted locator lights spaced at intervals in the aisle and exit indicators by each door. When illuminated, Escape Path Lighting provides visual guidance for emergency evacuation if all sources of lighting more than four feet above the aisle floor are obscured by smoke. Battery powered exit lights are located at each cabin exit.

Photolum Emergency Lights

A photoluminescent floor path marking system is installed along the cabin aisle. The photoluminescent material, when excited by light, will glow and provide exit path guidance. At the exit, electrically operated lights and markers provide exit identification. The photoluminescent strips need to be properly charged. The table below contains charging information and can be used to determine how long the strips remain illuminated. For charging, the cabin ceiling and sidewall lights need to be on at full intensity, and the strips should not be covered or blocked.

Exterior Emergency Lighting

Exterior Emergency lights are located at each entry door and emergency door. Lights are also installed in each slide to illuminate the ground at the end of the slide. Exterior Emergency lights are located at each entry door and over-wing emergency exit door. Lights are also installed in each slide to illuminate the ground at the end of the slide.

PART | EMERGENCY EQUIPMENT

Words and Expressions

interior [in'tɪərɪə]　　*n.* 内部，内景
　　　　　　　　　　　adj. 内部的，内的
exterior [ɪks'tɪərɪə]　　*n.* 外部，外面
　　　　　　　　　　　adj. 外面的，外部的
aisle [aɪl]　　*n.* 过道，通道
alternate ['ɔːltə(r)neɪt]　　*adj.* 轮流的；交替的
　　　　　　　　　　　vt. & vi. （使）交替；轮流
illuminate [ɪ'ljuːmɪneɪt]　　*vt. & vi.* 照亮，照明；照亮
disruption [dɪs'rʌpʃən]　　*n.* 分裂，瓦解；破裂，毁坏；中断
luminescent [ˌluːmɪ'nesnt]　　*adj.* 发冷光的，发光的
obscure [əb'skjuə]　　*adj.* 晦涩的，不清楚的
　　　　　　　　　　　vt. 使……模糊不清，掩盖；隐藏
photoluminescent　发光
strip [strɪp]　　*n.* 长条，条板；带状地带

Technical Terms

hot battery bus　　　　　　热电汇流条
luminescent exit sign　　　　发光出口指示牌
photoluminescent strip　　　撤离路线指示灯

Notes

1. The switch can be used to manually activate or arm the system for automatic operation.（应急灯光）开关用来手动开启或预位。

2. When illuminated, Escape Path Lighting provides visual guidance for emergency evacuation if all sources of lighting more than four feet above the aisle floor are obscured by smoke. 开始发光的时候，就算烟雾遮挡住地板四英尺上的光源，撤离路线指示灯也能为应急撤离提供目视引导。

Exercises

Ⅰ. Please answer the following questions.

1. What does the emergency lighting system consist of?
2. What are the features of different emergency lighting?

PART II

EMERGENCY PROCEDURES

PART II EMERGENCY PROCEDURES

CHAPTER 3
GENERAL INFORMATION FOR IN-FLIGHT EMERGENCY

Abnormal/emergency procedures are actions that must be taken by the cabin crew after a failure. Abnormal/emergency procedures, specific to the cabin crew, concern smoke/fire fighting, depressurization, etc.

The most important function of each crew member is to provide the greatest amount of safety to their customers. Safety extends from the prevention and care of the most minor mishaps to the more serious emergency situations that might arise.

Only those who have a firm understanding and working knowledge of emergency and standard procedures will be able to handle each emergency situation successfully and with a calm, confident, authoritative attitude. Anytime a crew member is incapacitated, his/her duties are the responsibility of the remaining crew.

In that no two emergencies are exactly alike, the procedures given here are intended primarily as guidelines and in no way should restrict the use of the flight attendant's own personal judgment and initiative. The procedures may be modified as you feel necessary.

When an irregular cabin situation occurs that is a safety hazard to the flight and/or customers, follow the chain of command. The purpose of a "chain of command" is to determine who the decision makers are during both routine and emergency situation.

The chain of command, in priority, is as follows:

–Captain

–First Officer

–"A" Flight Attendant

–"B" Flight Attendant

–"C" Flight Attendant

Notification of Captain

–Four rings to the flight deck indicate a cabin emergency situation.

–Captain will answer the interphone.

–Give as complete an assessment of the situation as possible.

–Continue to keep advised.

In-flight Operational Occurrence Report

–Complete and turn in to a supervisor within 24 hours after the termination of that sequence.

–Turn in immediately upon request from in-flight management.

–Give a factual statement of the occurrence.

Press or News Media

Do not make any written or verbal statement to the press or news media without prior briefing or approval from a member of the airlines management.

Words and Expressions

abnormal [æbˈnɔːməl]　　*adj.* 反常的，异常的；不规则的

PART II EMERGENCY PROCEDURES

mishap ['mɪsˌhæp]   *n.* 灾祸；不幸事故
authoritative [ɔːˈθɔrɪtətɪv]   *adj.* 权威的；有权力的；当局的；命令式的
initiative [ɪˈnɪʃɪətɪv]   *n.* 主动性；主动权
　　　　　　　　　　adj. 自发的；初步的
routine [ruːˈtiːn]   *n.* 例行公事；日常工作
　　　　　　　　　　adj. 例行的；常规的；日常的
interphone [ˈɪntə(ː)fəʊn]   *n.* 对讲机，内话机
assessment [əˈsesmənt]   *n.* 评估；评价
occurrence [əˈkʌrəns]   *n.* 发生，出现；遭遇，事件

Technical Terms

interphone 内话机

Notes

1. Abnormal/emergency procedures are actions that must be taken by the cabin crew after a failure. 应急程序是客舱乘务员在机上紧急情况发生时所必须采取的措施。

2. Give as complete an assessment of the situation as possible. 对（机上紧急）情况做出尽可能完整的评估。

3. In that no two emergencies are exactly alike, the procedures given here are intended primarily as guidelines and in no way should restrict the use of the flight attendant's own personal judgment and initiative. 因为没有任何两个应急情况是绝对相同的，本书给出的程序主要作为参考，并且绝对不能限制乘务员自身个人判断和主动性的发挥。

Exercises

Please answer the following questions.

1. What are the basic principles of handling the emergency in flight?
2. What is the "chain of command"?

PART Ⅱ EMERGENCY PROCEDURES

CHAPTER 4 INFLIGHT EMERGENCY

Section 1 Turbulence

Weather conditions can cause turbulence in the air which can affect the flight of the aircraft. These turbulent conditions vary in intensity and are classified as light, moderate, severe, or extreme.

Light turbulence is a condition during which occupants may be required to use seatbelts, but objects in the aircraft remain at rest. Light turbulence momentarily causes slight, erratic changes in the aircraft altitude or attitude. Passengers may feel a slight strain against seat belts. Liquids are shaking but are not splashing out of cups. Trolleys can be maneuvered with little difficulty.

Moderate turbulence is a condition during which occupants of the aircraft require seat belts and are occasionally thrown against the belt. Unsecured objects in the aircraft will be moved about. Moderate turbulence causes rapid bumps or jolts. Passengers feel definite strain against seat belts. Liquids are splashing out of cups. Trolleys are difficult to maneuver. It is difficult to walk or stand in the cabin.

Severe turbulence may cause the aircraft to be momentarily out of control. Occupants are thrown violently against the seat belt and back into their seats. Unsecured objects in the aircraft will be tossed about. Severe turbulence causes large abrupt changes in the aircraft altitude and attitude. Passengers are forced violently against their seatbelts. Items fall or lift off the floor. Loose items are tossed about the cabin.

Extreme turbulence is rarely encountered. When it occurs, the aircraft is violently tossed about and is extremely difficult to control. Structural damage may result.

Procedures to Follow During Turbulence

Unanticipated

During the flight, the aircraft may encounter areas of turbulence that were not forecast. For example, Clear Air Turbulence (CAT), which usually occurs at high altitudes, during cruise the aircraft, may suddenly enter an area of turbulence. Clear Air Turbulence can be forecast but cannot be detected by the aircraft radar, so there is often no warning. When other than tight turbulence is encountered unexpectedly, flight attendant should immediately take the nearest seat or jump seat and fasten seat belt and shoulder harness if on jump seat, then direct customers to fasten their seat belts. If one is in the galley, do not take time to secure galleys. Flight attendants should also remain seated until notified by the flight deck. If, in your opinion, a lengthy time has passed without turbulence, and you have received no instructions from the flight deck, you may use the interphone if on a jump seat, and request information.

Anticipated

The flight crew should be briefed on the en-route weather as part of the preparation for the flight. Therefore, the flight crew can be aware of possible areas of turbulence that are forecast for the flight. When notified by the captain that turbulence is anticipated, flight attendants should coordinate with flight deck by passenger announcement, advising customers of the situation and to fasten their seat belts securely. Then visually check customers to be sure their seat belts are fastened. Secure all loose items in the cabin and galley, after that take your flight attendant jump seat and fasten seat belt and shoulder harness. Flight attendants should also remain seated until notified by the flight deck. Check customers and cabin upon notification from flight deck. If, in your opinion, a lengthy time has passed without turbulence, and you have received no instructions from the flight deck, you may use the interphone if on a jump seat, and request information.

Cabin Management

It is possible that loose objects, such as passenger baggage, or service equipment, such as trays, trolleys, etc. become projectiles, and cause injury to cabin crewmembers and passengers during turbulence.

Operators should develop and implement strategies to enable the cabin crew to efficiently manage the cabin, in order to ensure safety and prevent turbulence-related injuries. Some practices can be applied to assist the cabin crew. Ensure that trolleys do not remain unattended in front of exits, outside the galleys, or in the aisles during cabin service. Frequently check the cabin during the flight to ensure that: the cabin is kept tidy, in order to limit the amount of loose objects, such as glasses and trays; passenger baggage is not left in the aisles; all the overhead stowage compartments are closed during the flight.

If the cabin crew implements the above-mentioned strategies, they will need less time to secure the cabin in the case of turbulence.

Galley Management

Many cabin crew injuries occur in the galley areas. These injuries are mostly due to galley equipment or objects that are not secured. Trolleys remain in the galleys without the brakes, for instance. Galley compartments are not correctly closed and latched, falling from their stowage, and spilling their contents. Bottles, coffee pots, and service items are falling of the galley countertops.

After each service, the cabin crew should stow trolleys in their correct stowage; set the trolley brake to ON, when the trolley is not being moved; close and lock the doors of trolleys and stowage compartments immediately after each use; stow service equipments that are not in use; stow service equipments that are in use in a drawer so that it can be easily stowed in the event of turbulence; use the latches provided on coffee/beverage makers to keep coffee pots secured in order to prevent hot contents from spilling.

Passenger Management

The most effective way to prevent passenger and cabin crew injuries during turbulence is to "sit down and buckle up". The best way to help prevent turbulence-related injury is to use seat belts. The flight crew and cabin crew should encourage the use of seat belts and the importance of passenger compliance with the FASTEN SEAT BELT signs.

Words and Expressions

intensity [ɪnˈtensɪti]　　*n.* 强烈，剧烈

turbulence [ˈtəːbjələns]　　*n.* 乱流

countertop [ˈkaʊntəˌtɒp]　　*n.* （厨房的）工作台面

trolley [ˈtrɒli]　　*n.* （两轮或四轮的）手推车

latch [lætʃ]　　*n.* （门窗的）门闩

spill [spɪl]　　*vt. & vi.* 溢出；泼出

toss about　翻来覆去

Technical Terms

light turbulence　　　　　　　　轻度颠簸

PART II *EMERGENCY PROCEDURES*

moderate turbulence 中度颠簸
severe turbulence 重度颠簸
extreme turbulence 极度颠簸
Clear Air turbulence 晴空颠簸

Notes

1. When other than tight turbulence is encountered unexpectedly, flight attendant should immediately take the nearest seat or jump seat and fasten seat belt and shoulder harness if on jump seat, then direct customers to fasten their seat belts. 如果遇到突如其来的颠簸，乘务员应该立刻坐到最近的座位或乘务员座席，并系好安全带和肩带（如果是乘务员座席），然后指导乘客系紧他们的安全带。

2. If, in your opinion, a lengthy time has passed without turbulence, and you have received no instructions from the flight deck, you may use the interphone if on a jump seat, and request information. 如果在你看来，很长时间过去没有再遇到颠簸，也没有收到来自驾驶舱的任何指令，这时你可以通过内话机（如果你坐在乘务员座席上）与驾驶舱取得联系，获得信息。

3. It is possible that loose objects, such as passenger baggage, or service equipment, such as trays, trolleys, etc. become projectiles, and cause injury to cabin crewmembers and passengers during turbulence. 在遇到颠簸时，松散的物件如乘客行李，或者是服务设备，如托盘、推车等，都有可能被抛出，对乘务员和乘客造成伤害。

4. These injuries are mostly due to galley equipment or objects that are not secured. 这些伤害大部分是由厨房设备或物件没有被固定好所造成的。

5. The most effective way to prevent passenger and cabin crew injuries during turbulence is to "sit down and buckle up". 在颠簸过程中，最有效的避免乘客和机组人员受伤的措施便是"坐下，系紧安全带"。

Exercises

Please answer the following questions.

1. How many kinds of turbulence are mentioned in the text and what are they?
2. If encountering an unanticipated turbulence, what should be done?
3. What should be frequently checked in the cabin during the flight?

Section 2 Slow Air Leaks

During the flight, it's unexpected to encounter slow air leak sometimes, which will cause great affect to the whole flight if it is not managed in time.

If there is slow air leak, you should report any air leaks to the flight deck. If flight deck is advised, reseat customers away from the air leak. If the air leak is from an exit that is next to the flight attendant jump seat, the flight attendant should sit in a customer seat for landing. Select a customer seat that will allow you to reach the exit before any customer can do so. Do not place any articles in the source of the leak. For the occupants, hypoxic symptoms may be experienced. If slow air leak is not noticed or handled, a decompression of the cabin may result.

If there is anything unusual, such as sounds or sighting, flight attendant should report any unusual sounds or sightings that you notice or your customers report to the flight deck, for example, anything out of the ordinary, thumping, hissing, ice on wings etc.

Words and Expressions

leak [li:k]   *vi.& vt.* 漏出；透露；使泄露
              n. 泄漏，漏洞

PART Ⅱ EMERGENCY PROCEDURES

reseat [ˌriːˈsiːt]　　*vt.* 使（自己或别人）再次就座；为……设新座位
article [ˈɑːtɪkl]　　*n.* 文章，论文；条款；物品
hypoxic [haɪˈpɒksɪk]　　*adj.* [医]含氧量低的
symptom [ˈsɪmptəm]　　*n.* 症状；征兆
thump [θʌmp]　　*vt. & vi.* 重击，捶击；砰地撞到
　　　　　　　　n. 砰的重击声；重击
hiss [hɪs]　　*v.* 发嘶嘶声；发出嘘声
　　　　　　n. 嘘声；嘶嘶声

Technical Terms

jump seat　　　　　　　（乘务员）弹跳座椅
flight deck　　　　　　驾驶舱
ice on wings　　　　　机翼结冰

Notes

1. If flight deck is advised, reseat customers away from the air leak. 得到驾驶舱的通知，重新安排乘客座位，远离漏气区域。
2. Select a customer seat that will allow you to reach the exit before any customer can do so. 乘务员在客舱选择座位的原则：离出口最近的座位。
3. Do not place any articles in the source of the leak. 漏气的地方不能放置任何物品。

Exercises

Please answer the following questions.

1. What is the basic procedure of handling slow air leak in flight?
2. If there is anything unusual, what should the flight attendant do at first hand?

Section 3 Cabin Decompression

Aircraft have cabin air systems that control pressurization, airflow, air filtration, and temperature. The purpose of these systems is to provide a safe and comfortable cabin environment, and to protect all cabin occupants from the physiological risks of high altitudes. Modern aircraft are now operating at increasingly high altitudes. This increases the physiological risks that are associated with decompression.

In the case of decompression, there is a risk that not enough oxygen will be supplied to the body. This condition, hypoxia, is the greatest threat to both crewmembers and passengers.

Types of Decompression

The risk of a pressurized cabin is the potential for cabin decompression. It can occur due to a pressurization system malfunction, or damage to the aircraft that causes a breach in the aircraft structure, enabling cabin air to escape outside the aircraft, for example, the loss of a window, or a breach in the aircraft fuselage due to an explosion.

The loss of pressurization can be slow in case of a small air leak while a rapid or explosive decompression occurs suddenly, usually within a few seconds.

The consequences of decompression and its impact on cabin occupants depends on a number of factors, including:

The size of the cabin–the larger the cabin, the longer the decompression time;

The damage to the aircraft structure–the larger the opening, the faster the decompression time;

The pressure differential–the greater the pressure differential between the

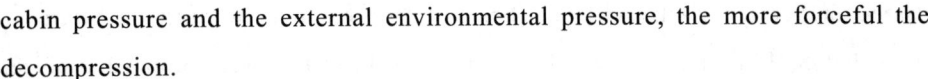

PART Ⅱ   *EMERGENCY PROCEDURES*

cabin pressure and the external environmental pressure, the more forceful the decompression.

When cabin pressure decreases, cabin occupants are no longer protected from the dangers of high altitudes, and there is an increased risk of hypoxia, decompression, illness, and hypothermia. It is, therefore, important that crewmembers recognize the different types of decompression, react effectively to overcome the difficulties associated with a loss in cabin pressure.

Rapid/Explosive Decompression

Rapid/Explosive decompression results in a sudden loss in cabin pressure and can be recognized by the following signs. A loud bang, thump or clap that is the result of the sudden contact between the internal and external masses of air; cloud of fog or mist in the cabin that is due to the drop in temperature and the change of humidity; rush of air, as the air exits the cabin; a decrease in temperature, as the cabin temperature equalizes with the outside air temperature; the release of the cabin oxygen masks, when the cabin altitude reaches 14,000 feet; loose items may become projectiles; dust particles may limit visibility. If a breach in the aircraft structure is the cause of the decompression, unsecured items in the immediate area are ejected from the aircraft; debris may fly around the cabin.

In the case of rapid/explosive decompression, there may be a lot of confusion due to the high noise level and fog that make it difficult to communicate in the cabin.

Slow/Insidious Decompression

Slow/Insidious decompression involves a very gradual decrease in cabin pressure. Slow decompression may be the result of a faulty door seal, a malfunction in the pressurization system, or a cracked window.

Slow decompression may not always be obvious. The cabin crew may not notice the changes in the cabin, until the oxygen masks drop down from the

Passenger Service Units (PSUs). Therefore, the cabin crew must be aware of signs that could indicate a slow decompression. In some cases, an unusual noise, such as whistling or hissing sound around the door areas, may be an indication of a slow decompression; therefore the flight crew should be notified immediately.

One of the first physiological indications of a slow decompression may be ear discomfort or "popping", joint pain, or stomach pain due to gas expansion.

Physical Changes to the Cabin Environment and Customers

Explosive noise is followed by a rapid movement of cabin air toward the hole. Rush of air will carry with it paper, loose clothing, dirt and other light objects lying in its path. There is a sudden decrease in cabin air temperature. The cabin becomes foggy due to moisture condensation in the expanding cabin atmosphere.

The physiological symptoms of a decompression are headache, respiratory changes and difficulties, excessive sleepiness, light headed or dizzy sensations, blue coloring of skin, lips, fingernails, indifference and a feeling of well-being, fatigue, deterioration of the sense, personality changes and unconsciousness.

In the flight deck, there is a warning system. The warning horn in the flight deck sounds when the cabin altitude reaches 14,000 feet. The "Fasten Seat Belt", "No Smoking", and lavatory "Return to Seat" signs will be turned on by the flight deck.

Procedures of Decompression

In the case of decompression the immediate use of oxygen is critical. Therefore, the first actions to be performed by the cabin crew are immediately donning the nearest oxygen mask, sitting down and fastening the seat belt, or grasping a fixed object and holding on.

If the cabin crew are not able to sit down or grasp a fixed object, they should wedge themselves between passengers and ask passengers for assistance. For example, in one cabin decompression event, a cabin crewmember was saved from ejection out of the aircraft, because a passenger was holding on to the cabin crewmember's ankle.

The priority of the cabin crew is to consider their personal safety. Incapacitated or injured cabin crewmembers will not be able to assist other cabin crewmembers and passengers during the post-decompression phase.

When decompression occurs, all flight attendants should immediately take oxygen from the nearest mask and secure themselves. While proceeding to the nearest available mask, flight attendants should give commands "USE OXYGEN MASK", "NO SMOKING", "FASTEN SEAT BELT". All must remain seated until advised by the captain that oxygen is no longer required. Flight attendant turns on the cabin lights to bright and then checks and assists passengers throughout the cabin with first aid portable oxygen bottles. Repacking the aircraft oxygen masks after the masks dropping is not allowed. Oxygen masks must be repacked by qualified personnel. Customers should place the mask over their nose and mouth and breathe normally. They should continue wearing the mask until advised by the crew.

Generation of the individual chemical units may cause a "burning" odor which may be easily mistaken for odors from a fire. In addition, the chemical canisters can become very hot. Caution should be taken to avoid touching any chemical generator.

Many incident and accident reports have revealed that effective crew communication, between flight and cabin crew, can make the difference between an accident and an incident. It has also been revealed that ineffective communication between the flight and cabin crew has contributed to the severity of an accident.

Cabin crews are trained to anticipate the occurrence of specific actions during specific events. In the case of decompression, it would be quite reasonable for the cabin crew to expect the flight crew to make an emergency descent. However, when the expected does not happen, how should the cabin crew react if the oxygen masks deploy and the aircraft continues to climb?

When a slow decompression is happening, the aircraft continues to climb. This type of scenario is rare. However it is important to consider how the cabin crew should react in this type of event. In this case, the cabin crewmember seating closest to the cockpit, should immediately notify the flight crew of the oxygen mask deployment, and also confirm that the flight crew have donned their oxygen masks.

When the expected does not happen, the cabin crew must take the initiative to seek and find an explanation. If the cabin crew suspect that the safety of the flight is at risk, or that there is any indication of an abnormal situation, the cabin crew must immediately notify the flight crew.

In the case of rapid/explosive decompression, the level of noise will be very high. Therefore, it makes communication difficult between the flight crew and the cabin crew, and equally between the cabin crew and the passengers. Due to the fact that effective communication is vital during any emergency, the cabin crew should use any available form of communication. For example, in several accidents involving rapid/explosive decompression, cabin and flight crews were forced to communicate via hand signals and gestures. Cabin crewmembers must, therefore, be prepared to improvise and use the imagination.

After a decompression, when the aircraft reaches a safe altitude, the cabin crew can move around the cabin, and should use the portable oxygen cylinders until they are confident that they can breathe without support. When the emergency descent is completed, and a safe altitude is reached, the cabin crew should consider their oxygen requirements. Due to the physical activity at an increased altitude, the cabin crew may still be exposed to hypoxia. Oxygen deprivation can be insidious and the cabin crew may not be the best judges of their own oxygen intake after decompression. After cabin decompression, the cabin crew should check on the flight crew, and be prepared to assist in the case of pilot incapacitation, check passengers for any injuries, check the cabin for any damage, provide first-aid and oxygen as necessary and report the cabin status to the flight crew as soon as possible.

During any emergency, effective crew communication is critical to a successful outcome. Effective Crew Resource Management (CRM) involves cooperation and communication between the flight and cabin crew. In many abnormal and emergency situations, the cabin crew play an important role in helping the flight crew to identify and resolve developing problems.

Words and Expressions

decompression [ˌdi:kəmˈpreʃən]　*n.* 减压，解压
altitude [ˈæltɪtjuːd]　*n.* 高度，海拔
hypoxia [haɪˈpɒksɪə]　*n.* 组织缺氧，氧不足
hypothermia [ˌhaɪpəˈθɜːmɪə]　*n.* 低体温
associate [əˈsəʊʃɪeɪt]　*vt. & vi.* （使）发生联系，（使）联合；结交，结伙
eject from　用力将……从（某处）投〔喷〕出
insidious [ɪnˈsɪdiːəs] *adj.* 隐伏的，潜在的，暗中为害的
malfunction [mælˈfʌŋkʃən] *n.* 故障，障碍
hissing [ˈhɪsɪŋ]　*n.* 发嘶嘶声，蔑视
moisture [ˈmɔɪstʃə]　*n.* 水分，水气，湿气
　　　　　　　　　vt. 使防潮
deterioration [dɪˌtɪrɪəˈreɪʃən]　*n.* 变坏,堕落；衰退
sensation [senˈseɪʃən]　*n.* 感觉，感受
phase [feɪz]　*n.* 阶段，时期
don [dɒn]　*vt.* 穿上，披上
deprivation [ˌdeprəˈveɪʃən]　*n.* 剥夺；被夺去，丧失
status [ˈsteɪtəs,ˈstætəs] *n.* 情形，状况；身份，地位

Technical Terms

pressurization system malfunction　　增压系统故障
cabin decompression　　客舱释压
rapid decompression　　快速释压
slow decompression　　缓慢释压
emergency descent　　紧急下降
crew resource management　　机组资源管理

Notes

1. Aircraft have cabin air systems that control pressurization, airflow, air filtration, and temperature. 飞机有客舱气压系统，控制着客舱的增压、气流、空气过滤及温度。

2. In the case of decompression, there is a risk that not enough oxygen will be supplied to the body. This condition, hypoxia, is the greatest threat to both crewmembers and passengers. 如果遇到客舱释压，危险在于不再有充足的氧气提供给身体。组织缺氧这种情况，对于乘务员和乘客来说都是最大的威胁。

3. In the case of decompression the immediate use of oxygen is critical. 如果遇到客舱释压，紧急用氧是至关重要的。

4. the release of the cabin oxygen masks, when the cabin altitude reaches 14,000 feet 当客舱高度达到 14 000 英尺，氧气面罩会放出。
注：客舱高度和飞行高度有区别。客舱高度也叫座舱高度，是指增压后的客舱气压高度，表示的是压力；而飞行高度是指在空中至某一基准水平面的垂直距离。

5. Slow/Insidious decompression involves a very gradual decrease in cabin pressure. 缓慢（潜在）性释压指客舱逐渐失去客舱压力。

6. In some cases an unusual noise, such as whistling or hissing sound around the door areas, may be an indication of a slow decompression; therefore the flight crew should be notified immediately. 在某些情况下，异乎寻常的噪音，诸如舱门周围区域发出的口哨声或嘶嘶声，都有可能是缓慢释压的征兆；因此，乘务员需要及时地被告知这些情况。
7. The priority of the cabin crew is to consider their personal safety. 乘务员最优先考虑的事是自身安全。
8. Crew Resource Management (CRM) involves cooperation and communication between the flight and cabin crew. 机组资源管理包括飞行机组和乘务组之间的配合和沟通。

Exercises

Please answer the following questions.

1. How many types of decompression are mentioned in the text?
2. What is the priority of the cabin crew when encounter a decompression?
3. When cabin crew suspect that the safety of the flight is at risk, what should they do?
4. What should cabin crew do after a decompression?

Section 4　Cabin Smoke

The smoke in cabin may come from different source. They are mainly of three types: from electrical, from air conditioning, from cabin equipment. It is attempted to classify the different cabin smoke origins according to their characteristics: one is easy-to-identify smoke origin, and another is hard-to-identify.

Easy-to-identify cabin smoke origin includes lavatory smoke, crew rest compartment smoke (A330/A340), VCC smoke. The main characteristics of these types of smoke warnings are they are always covered by an ECAM and FAP (Forward Attendant Panel) warnings and procedure. This includes also passenger seat, galley odour and/or smoke coming from water boiler, microwave oven, coffeemaker, which are not covered by an ECAM/FAP warnings. For these cabin smoke origins, the crew always have the same approach: locate the smoke, pull circuit breaker (for galley, oven…), and switch off the commercial cabin switch (PAX SYS, COMMERCIAL…), isolate the smoke by closing the door/exit hatch, close isolation valve and apply the fire fighting procedure (manual or extinguishing system).

Hard-to-identify cabin smoke origin concerns air conditioning smoke, and smoke coming from cabin lining. The characteristics of these types of smoke origin are that they are not covered by ECAM/FAP warnings and more difficult for the crew to locate and treat them.

The key factor of the procedures is time. Only a close communication between cabin crew and flight crew can save precious minutes in these uncomfortable situations. The first step of a cabin smoke procedure is the alert phase. As presented before, only a few cabin smoke sources are monitored in the cabin. Some alarms are available on ECAM and on the FAP but detectors are not installed everywhere. So the cabin crew's attention to any particular smoke or even smell is important.

In any case, if smoke is detected, the cabin crew must report to the flight crew what happens in the cabin, the density, and the severity of the smoke encountered. Even for smoke monitored area, the information concerning the smoke density is not given by the detectors. Only the cabin crew can inform the flight crew.

As soon as smoke has been detected, a few actions–so called common actions–are to be applied immediately by the flight crew whatever the origin of the smoke is, even before trying to determine the smoke origin. Basically, they consist in extracting of smoke overboard, stopping of cabin fan to avoid spreading of smoke in the cabin, galley extinguishing. This step aims at minimizing a further contamination of the cabin. Of course, if the faulty equipment is already identified, it must be isolated immediately.

Words and Expressions

odour ['əʊdə]   *n.* 气味；臭气
circuit ['sɜːkɪt]   *n.* 电路，线路
hatch [hætʃ]   *vt. & vi.* 孵化；秘密策划
                 n. 开口，活板门；舱口
alert [əˈlɜːt]   *adj.* 警惕的，警觉的，注意的
                vt. 使（某人）保持警觉
density ['densɪti]   *n.* 密集，稠密
faulty ['fɔːlti]   *adj.* 有错误的，有缺点的；出毛病的

Technical Terms

VCC	电源电压
FAP	前舱乘务员控制面板
ECAM	电子集中式飞机监控
isolation valve	隔离阀；隔离活门
circuit breaker	断路开关，断路器

Notes

1. The smoke in cabin may come from different sources. They are mainly of three types: from electrical, from air conditioning, from cabin equipment. 客舱产生的烟有不同的来源，大概分为三个类型：电力、空调和客舱设备。

2. In any case, if smoke is detected, the cabin crew must report to the flight crew what happens in the cabin, the density, and the severity of the smoke encountered. 在任何情况下，如果客舱有烟被探测到，乘务组必须向飞行机组做出汇报：客舱里发生了什么、烟的浓度以及严重程度。

Exercises

Please answer the following questions.

1. What's the classification of the cabin smoke origins?
2. What should be done when smoke is detected?

Section 5 Fire Prevention Awareness

Awareness is the flight attendant's most valuable tool for preventing in-flight fires. All articles that may contribute to the cause of a fire, such as matches, must be properly stowed so as to lessen the risk of unintentional ignition.

On designated flights where smoking is permitted, (i.e. charter flights) the flight attendant must be aware of customers smoking in the aisle, be alert to customers entering lavatories with cigarettes, and watch for customers failing asleep while smoking.

When reporting any indications of a potential problem, clearly define the area of the smoke origin, density and odor. Give as much information as possible.

Basic Fire Chemistry

To enable cabin crew to effectively fight an in-flight fire, it is important for cabin crew to have a basic knowledge of fire chemistry. This will help cabin crew to understand the importance of selecting the correct fire extinguisher in a given fire situation.

The key to fire prevention is keeping fuel and ignition sources separate.

Combustion consists of three elements: oxygen, heat, and fuel. Together, these elements create a chemical chain reaction and result in a fire. The goal of firefighting is to eliminate at least one element from the fire, in order to extinguish it. A fire will continue, unless the fuel supply has been cut off, or there is no more oxygen available or the temperature has been cooled below the flammability temperature.

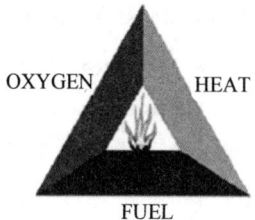

Figure 4.1

Classification of Fires

Class A fires involve wood, paper, cloth, or plastic. Class A fires need to be cooled. A water extinguisher, or liquid containing a large percentage of water, for example, coffee, tea and juice will extinguish a class A fires. Do not use liquid containing alcohol! Water/glycol extinguishers are the most effective for class A fires. The smoke is usually gray/brown in color, which can be quite thick, depending on the quantity of fuel.

 CLASS A

Figure 4.2

Class B fires involve flammable liquid, hydraulic fluid, oil, tar or aircraft fuel. This type of fire can not be extinguished with water. Foam or Halon fire extinguishers should be used to extinguish class B fires. The smoke is usually black in color, and it's very

 CLASS B

Figure 4.3

thick, with a distinct oil/petrol-like odor.

Class C fires involve electrical equipment. This type of fire must be extinguished with a non-conducting mixture, in order to avoid electrocution and damage to electrical circuitry. Halon fire extinguishers are effective for class C fires. The smoke is usually light grey or white, with a bluish tinge. It is very fine and can disperse rapidly. It has a distinct acrid odor.

Figure 4.4

Class D fires involve flammable metals, such as sodium, magnesium, lithium and potassium. Special powder extinguishers are effective on class D fires, because of the possible chemical reaction between the burning and extinguishing agents. Never use Halon fire extinguishers on class D fires.

Figure 4.5

Crew Communication and Coordination

In the event of an in-flight fire, communication between the cabin crew and flight crew is essential. If a fire is discovered in the cabin, the cabin crew must inform the flight crew immediately. The firefighting effort requires coordination amongst the cabin crew. The duties are divided into three main roles, the firefighter, the communicator, the assistant firefighter. All other cabin crewmembers play supporting roles.

The first cabin crewmember that finds the fire will assume the role of the firefighter. The firefighter should alert other cabin crewmembers first. Then take the nearest appropriate fire extinguisher and immediately locate the source of the fire and extinguish the fire.

The second cabin crewmember on the scene is in charge of the communicating information about the fire. This cabin crewmember is called the communicator. The communicator should inform the flight crew of the fire location, fire source, severity/density of fire and/or smoke (color of smoke/odor), the time the firefighting action started, firefighting progress and the number of fire extinguishers used. He/she must maintain the communication link between the cabin and the flight crew via an interphone near the firefighting scene, providing the flight crew with an accurate description of the firefighting effort, and of the situation in the cabin.

The third cabin crewmember on the scene assumes the assistant firefighter role. The assistant firefighter provides additional firefighting equipment to support the firefighting effort. He/she can help removing flammable materials from the area, and must be prepared to replace the firefighter, and change roles with the firefighter, if required.

Other cabin crewmembers, who are not directly involved in the firefighting effort, are required to provide assistance, such as relocating passengers, providing first-aid and calming and reassuring passengers.

After any fire or smoke occurrence, one cabin crewmember should be responsible for monitoring the affected area for the remainder of the flight, and for regularly reporting to the purser. Then the purser will report to the flight crew.

Here are some tips of fighting a fire in the flight:

—Report any uncertain cabin smoke to the flight deck immediately.

—Attempt to locate the source of smoke. A PBE may be useful.

—If fire is present, classify fire.

—Fight the fire with the nearest appropriate fire extinguisher and remove electrical galley power as applicable.

—Have additional firefighting equipment available.

—Another flight attendant should simultaneously notify the captain, (4 rings) and maintain communication throughout the incident.

—Inspect area thoroughly to ensure extinguishment. A H_2O extinguisher or other liquids may be used on a class "A" fire.

—Advise customers to stay seated unless it is necessary to move some customers away from smoke, fumes or flames.

—Instruct customers to breathe through clothing or wet paper towels brought up around the face.

—A customer requiring oxygen due to smoke inhalation should be reseated away from the fire-affected area.

Words and Expressions

lessen [ˈles(ə)n]　*vt. & vi* 变少，减少（某事物）

unintentional [ˌʌnɪnˈtenʃənl]　*adj.* 不是故意的，无心的，无意识的

ignition [ɪgˈnɪʃən]　*n.* 点火，着火，引燃

combustion [kəmˈbʌstʃən]　*n.* 燃烧，烧毁

eliminate [ɪˈlɪmɪneɪt]　*vt.* 消除，排除

alcohol [ˈælkəˌhɒl]　*n.* 酒；酒精；含酒精的饮料

glycol [ˈglaɪkɒl]　*n.* 乙二醇

tar [tɑ:]　*n.* 焦油，沥青，柏油

disperse [dɪsˈpɜ:s]　*vt.* （使）分散，（使）散开

circuitry [ˈsɜ:kɪtri]　*n.* 电路，线路

bluish [ˈblu:ɪʃ]　*adj.* 浅蓝色的，带青色的

tinge [tɪndʒ]　*n.* 轻微的色泽，色度；气息，风味；味道

sodium [ˈsəʊdɪəm]　*n.* [化]钠

magnesium [mægˈni:zɪəm, -ʒəm]　*n.* [化]镁（金属元素）

lithium [ˈlɪθɪəm]　*n.* 锂

potassium [pəˈtæsɪəm]　*n.* 钾

Technical Terms

charter flight	包机
in-flight fire	机上火灾
flammable liquid	可燃液体
hydraulic fluid	液压液

PART II EMERGENCY PROCEDURES

Notes

1. The key to fire prevention is keeping fuel and ignition sources separate. 预防火灾的关键在于将燃料和点燃装置分开。
2. The duties are divided into three main roles, the firefighter, the communicator, the assistant firefighter; all other cabin crewmembers play a supporting role.（灭火）的职责被分为三个主要的部分：灭火员、通讯员、协助灭火员。其余的客舱乘务员起着支援的作用。
3. After any fire or smoke occurrence, one cabin crewmember should be responsible for monitoring the affected area for the remainder of the flight, and for regularly reporting to the purser. 在任何一次客舱起火或客舱冒烟的情况发生之后，一名乘务员将负责监控起火（冒烟）区域，并且在剩余航程中不间断地向乘务长进行汇报。
4. A customer requiring oxygen due to smoke inhalation should be reseated away from the fire-affected area. 因为吸入烟而需要使用氧气的乘客需要重新安置座位，远离火灾发生区域。
   注：重新安置乘客座位要考虑飞机配平。

Exercises

I. Please answer the following questions.

1. When reporting any indications of a potential problem, what should be included?
2. What elements do the combustion consist of?
3. What are the features of Class A fire?
4. What are the features of Class C fire? Which kind of fire extinguisher is effective for this type of fire?
5. How many roles are there in a fire fighting process? What are the duties for each role?

II. Focusing on Practice

Objective:

Master the organization of the roles in the fire fighting process.

Suggestions:

Practice can be fullfilled through grouping in the class. All the process should be timed and monitored by the group leader or the instructor.

Section 6　Area Specific Fires

Fires in Hidden Areas

Cabin crewmembers should be aware that hidden fires can occur in areas that are not visible or easily accessible to the cabin crew. There are areas on the aircraft where fires may propagate undetected in hidden areas, sidewalls, ceiling panels, floors.

Indications of a fire in a hidden area may be an unusually hot surface, smoke emitted from a wall seams or ceiling panels, fumes and unusual odors and snapping, or popping noises, may indicate electrical arcing.

If the cabin crew suspect a fire in a hidden area, for example, behind a panel, try to locate a "hot spot", which is an unusually warm area. A "hot spot" generally is a good indicator as to where the source of the fire is. To find the "hot spot", move the back of the hand along the panel to find the hottest area. Use the back of the hand, because the skin on the back of the hand is thinner and is more sensitive to temperature changes than the palm.

It may be necessary to remove panels to access the hidden area, or to make an incision in a panel large enough to insert the nozzle of the extinguisher, to discharge the extinguishing agent. Cabin crew should consider the use of other equipment to remove panels; these items may include ice tongs, spoons, knives,

PART Ⅱ EMERGENCY PROCEDURES

scissors (from the first aid kit) and the manual release tool. When removing, or making incisions in panel, some of these areas may contain essential wiring or aircraft systems. Carefully lift, lever, or cut a panel.

Galley Smoke/Fire

If the smoke/electrical smell source (may be water boiler, oven, coffeemaker, refrigerator and chiller) is identified, cabin attendants should pull the applicable circuit breaker. The applicable circuit breakers are located on the galley's centralized electrical panel. Then the electrical power should be cut off.

If the smoke/electrical smell source cannot be identified, the galley should be shut off first. Then pull the main galley circuit breaker or pull all circuit breakers. The applicable circuit breakers are located on the galley's centralized electrical panel. If necessary, apply the smoke/ fire fighting procedure. Cabin crew should also inform cockpit crew as soon as possible.

Oven Fires

Oven fires are a common occurrence on board the aircraft. Many oven fires are preventable. Some of the contributing factors to oven fires have been items left in the oven such as paper towels, saran wrap.

When an oven fire occurs, the oven door should be kept closed. It is hazardous to open an oven door when a fire is present, because this will introduce oxygen and may cause flash fire.

In the case of an oven fire, the firefighter should take the following actions. First of all, keep the oven door closed to deprive the fire of oxygen. In most cases, the fire will extinguish by itself. And then, isolate the electrical power from the oven by pulling the corresponding circuit breaker and turning off the oven power. After that, one cabin crewmember should monitor the situation. What's more, a fire extinguisher, PBE, and fire gloves must be ready to use in case that the situation deteriorates.

If the situation worsens, or fire is still present, the firefighter should don the PBE and fire gloves for protection. Open the oven very slightly, just enough to insert the nozzle of the fire extinguisher. Then, insert the nozzle of the fire extinguisher, and discharge the extinguishing agent. Close the oven door. Repeat the procedure, if necessary.

Any time a galley circuit breaker pops, it should be reset only once. The Captain must be notified. If smoke or fire is evident, the Flight Attendant should first attempt to shut off electrical power from the galley by pulling the circuit breaker on the galley wall. If the galley master circuit breaker can not be pulled due to smoke or fire, request that the captain removes galley electrical power and specifies galley. Whenever fighting galley fire, always use the Halon fire extinguisher. Do not return galley power after any incident involving circuit breakers, without checking with the captain first.

Lavatory Fires

If the lavatory smoke detector is activated, the flight attendant will check the lavatory smoke detector for occupancy by knocking on the door and announcing "flight attendant has to enter". Feel the lavatory door with the back of the hand at different heights to estimate the intensity of a possible fire.

If the door is cool and the customer does not open the door, flight attendant should pause and open the door cautiously. If it is suspected that a customer has been smoking, here are some appropriate procedures. First, check for presence of smoke and/or fire (a PBE may be useful) in the trash can, which is under the sink and all other accessible compartments. Use fire fighting procedures as necessary and alert the captain and advise of the status.

If the door is moderately hot, open door cautiously (a PBE may be useful), extinguish contents of Halon into the lavatory, low to the floor and alert the captain and advise of the status.

PART Ⅱ EMERGENCY PROCEDURES

If the door is very hot, or fire is out of control, keep the lavatory door shut, advise the captain immediately and surround door and jump seat area with wet blankets. Flight attendants and customers may need to be reseated. Flight attendants will need to occupy a customer seat allowing closet accessibility to an exit.

Waste Bin Fire

If there is a fire in the waste bin, the fire extinguisher operates automatically. When a predetermined temperature has been reached, the fusible plug at the end of the discharge tube melts and enables the extinguishing agent to flow into the waste bin.

Cabin crew should ensure that a preflight check of the pressure gauge is conducted, to ensure that the waste bin fire extinguisher is functional. Regular check of the lavatories should be conducted in-flight as part of the cabin crew duties.

Seat Fires

This situation is rarely encountered. However, if it occurs, one can kick the seat back forward when possible, which helps inhibit the flame height. Then flight attendant should use the Halon extinguisher, following with a H_2O extinguisher to saturate.

Flash Fire

A flash fire may occur when fuel enters the aircraft through the right wing. The over wing window exits, especially aircraft right, will properly be unavailable and should be blocked off immediately. Remember when referring to an engine fire, engine #1 is aircraft left and engine #2 is aircraft right. In the event of an emergency such as a flash fire, common sense and good judgment will determine the necessary procedures. The "A" position flight attendant will start deplaning customers immediately through the forward entry door. The "B" and "C" flight attendants are to evaluate the situation and go to their assigned emergency exits if necessary. If exit is usable, proceed with evacuation of customers as quickly as possible. Escape slides are disarmed at this time and must be armed if they are to be used.

Fluorescent Light Ballast Fires

Most fluorescent light fires will self extinguish as they are caused by a burning of the gas inside the bulb cavity. Once the gas is "burned off", the fire risk is no longer present. If in such case, you should notify the captain, turn lights to "OFF" and use a Halon fire extinguisher if necessary.

APU torching

Torching is a burst of flames expelled from the aircraft's auxiliary power unit (APU). The occurrence is very similar to an auto mobile backfire. You will not see torching if it occurs on the 737 because the APU is at the tail of the aircraft. However, if you or one of your customers see a temporary burst of flames on another aircraft, you will be able to explain the occurrence and reassure them that everything is all right.

Words and Expressions

vent [vent]   *n.* 出口；喷口，通风口；排气孔

auxiliary [ɔːgˈzɪliəri]   *adj.* 辅助的，补充的；备用的

backfire [bækˈfaɪə]   *vi.* 逆火，回火

be expelled from 被……开除

functional [ˈfʌŋkʃənəl]   *adj.* 有用的；能起作用的，产生影响的

PART Ⅱ *EMERGENCY PROCEDURES*

predetermine [ˌpri:dɪ'tɜ:mɪn] *vt.* 预定，注定；预先决定……的方向；使先存偏见

flammability [ˌflæmɪ'bɪlətɪ] *n.* 易燃，可燃性

amongst [ə'mʌŋst] *prep.* （表示位置）处在……中，为……所环绕，为……所环抱

fume [fju:m] *n.* 烟雾，气味

flame [fleɪm] *n.* 火焰

incision [ɪn'sɪʒən] *n.* 切开；切口

centralize ['sentrəˌlaɪz] *vt.* 使……处于中央的控制之下，把……集中于中央

wrap [ræp] *vt.* 包，裹；卷

resume [rɪ'zju:m] *vt. & vi.* 重新开始；恢复

fusible ['fju:zəbl] *adj.* 熔解的，可熔的

saturate ['sætʃəreɪt] *vt.* 浸湿，浸透；使……大量吸收或充满某物

fluorescent [fluə'resnt] *adj.* 荧光的，发荧光的

ballast ['bæləst] *n.* （保持船身稳定的）压舱物

  vt. 给某物装上压舱物

Technical Terms

smoke detector	烟雾探测器
discharge tube	放电管
galley fire	厨房失火
oven fires	烤炉失火
lavatory fires	卫生间失火
waste bin fire	垃圾桶失火
seat fires	座椅失火
fluorescent light ballast	荧光灯整流器
APU	辅助动力装置

Notes

1. It may be necessary to remove panels to access the hidden area, or to make an incision in a panel large enough to insert the nozzle of the extinguisher, to discharge the extinguishing agent. 为了靠近起火的隐藏区域，有可能会移走隔板，或者在隔间上开一个灭火器喷嘴大小的切口，以便将灭火物质喷进去。

2. Feel the lavatory door with the back of the hand at different heights to estimate the intensity of a possible fire. 用手背去试卫生间门不同高度位置的温度，以此来估计火势的大小。

3. Any time a galley circuit breaker pops, it should be reset only once. The Captain must be notified. 任何时候厨房开关跳起，只能重置一次，并应将情况通知机长。

4. If there is a fire in the waste bin, the fire extinguisher operates automatically. 如果是（卫生间的）垃圾箱起火，旁边的灭火装置会自动启动。

   注：卫生间的垃圾箱安装有自动灭火装置。灭火瓶安装在垃圾箱板顶端。填注管向灭火器内加注海龙。每个垃圾箱斜槽装有一个温度指示器，当垃圾箱附近温度过高时会发出指示。温度达到约 79 摄氏度时，导管上的热熔帽熔化，释放装置将会启动，灭火瓶将在 60 秒内工作。

Exercises

Ⅰ. **Please answer the following questions.**

1. What are the differences between the oven fire fighting procedures and the lavatory fire fighting procedures?
2. What can be used when fighting a hidden area fire?

3. If a seat is on fire, what should be done?

4. Depending on different situations, what are the lavatory fire fighting procedures?

Ⅱ. Focusing on Practice

Objective:

Master the procedures of extinguishing the lavatory fires.

Master the procedures of extinguishing the oven fires

Suggestions:

Practice can be fullfilled through grouping in the class. All the process should be timed and monitored by the group leader or the instructor.

Section 7　Bomb and Sabotage Threats

The threat of a bombing or sabotage to an aircraft or facility has become a fact of life throughout the aviation industry. Experience has shown the great majority of threats are hoaxes and do not result in an actual bomb being found. However, airlines are responsible for the safety and comfort of all people on board an aircraft, making it necessary to evaluate all threats and respond accordingly. A serious threat is posed to the airline when there is possibility of an explosive on board, whether on the ground or in flight.

An in-flight crewmember must be prepared for three different types of threats. Direct Verbal Threats–threat being made by aggressor to company personnel. "There is a bomb on board." Indirect Communicated Threats–a threat made by means of written or telephone communication. Suspicious Objects–an alien object found on board the aircraft.

Upon receiving a bomb sabotage threat it will be classified as specific or non-specific. The threat will be classified as specific when one or more of the following factors are present.

Specific statement is made such as "the next flight departing, or arriving, from (a named airport) has a bomb on board." The origin and/or destination of a flight is given, an exact date and/or time is stated, a particular flight number is mentioned.

Bomb threat procedures are not quite the same during different phase of the flight. When the customer makes bomb threat while boarding, the cabin crew must immediately notify the captain and Airport Services Agent/Customer Service Supervisor of the situation for evaluation. The supervisor will request security as necessary. The flight attendant shouldn't divulge threat or information to other customers. Keep the person making the threat, or indicating knowledge of a bomb threat under surveillance until relieved by an airline representative or security personnel. Check with the captain and Airport Services Agent/Customer Service Supervisor for further instructions.

When the bomb threat is at the gate of the aircraft, the captain will coordinate with the Airport Services Agent/Customer Service Supervisor to determine the appropriate actions to be taken. Ensure that "A" position flight attendant is briefed on the following information: whether to deplane customers; the manner in which customers will deplane (i.e. airstrips or customer loading stairs); whether carry-on luggage should be removed from aircraft; whether flight attendants should perform cabin security check on deplane; coordinate a P.A. advising customers of situation. Then the "A" position flight attendant will brief "B" and "C" position flight attendants on the situation and procedures which should be followed. If instructed, the flight attendants will assist ground personnel escorting the customers to a suitable holding area.

When the bomb threat occurs during the aircraft maneuvering on the ground, the captain will coordinate with ground operations on a plan of action and inform the "A" position flight attendant of the threat and the action to be taken. Also, the method of deplaning customers will be instructed. Whether the carry-on baggage should be left on board will also be notified to the flight attendants.

PART II EMERGENCY PROCEDURES

Then coordinate appropriate P.A. to inform the customers of the procedure to be used for deplaning. When getting all these information, the "A" position flight attendant will brief "B" and "C" position flight attendants on the plan of action. When directed by the captain to deplane, the "C" position flight attendant will deplane first, taking a megaphone for use in assembling the customers in a safe area, at least 300 feet from the aircraft, ensure the customers to stay together in a group and absolutely no smoking unless authorized by the Captain. Any cabin duties of the "C" position flight attendant will be assumed by the "B" position flight attendant. The "A" and "B" flight attendants will conduct the deplaning of customers. If directed by the captain, the "A" and "B" position flight attendants should perform a cabin security check. Once off the aircraft, crewmembers should not make any statements to the press. The crew and customers should follow the instructions of the local authorities.

When the bomb threat is happening during the flight, the captain will evaluate all information received, and may select to continue to the original destination, or return to the point of departure, even divert to a suitable alternate. The captain will coordinate a plan of action with Ground Operations, and inform the "A" flight attendant of the situation and the method for deplaning customers. The captain will also coordinate with the "A" position flight attendant any appropriate P.A. announcements. The "A" position flight attendant will brief "B", "C" and "D" position flight attendants on the situation and the plan of action to be taken. Upon landing, the aircraft will proceed to the designated dispersal area directed by the tower and follow bomb threat-aircraft maneuvering on the ground procedures.

When any bomb, explosive device is found on board the flight, assume you are dealing with a live device and notify the captain immediately! The captain is at complete and full command. His or her judgment and decisions are absolute and final. It is up to the captain as to whether the device should be left in place. If it is left in place, use the following procedures: move customers as far away from the device as possible. If there are empty seats, readjust the seating; DON'T cut any string or tape which is under tension; DON'T open any closed containers which are suspectful; DON'T disconnect or cut any wires or electrical connections; keep the device in the exact place and in the attitude in which it is found. Stabilize it in this position so it will not be able to move during descent and landing; reduce fragmentation and fire potential as much as possible; carefully pile blankets and pillows around the device; deplane customers following instructions of the captain.

Words and Expressions

sabotage ['sæbətɑ:ʒ]　*n.* 阴谋破坏
　　　　　　　　　　vt. 阴谋破坏（某事物）
aggressor [ə'gresə]　*n.* 侵略者
verbal ['vəbəl]　*adj.* 词语的，言语的；口头的
hoax [həuks]　*n.* 恶作剧；戏弄
　　　　　　　vt. 开玩笑骗某人；戏弄某人
pose [pəuz]　*vt.* 提出；使摆姿势；以……身份出现
supervisor ['sjupə,vaɪzə]　*n.* 监督者，管理者
surveillance [sə'veləns]　*n.* 监督，管制
deplane [dɪ'plen]　*v.* （使）下飞机
airstrip ['eə,strɪp]　*n.* 飞机跑道
readjust [rɪə'dʒʌst]　*vt. & vi.* 再整理，再调整
dispersal [dɪ'spəsəl]　*n.* 散布，分散，消散，驱散，疏散

Technical Terms

suspicious object　　　　　机上可疑物品
airport services agent　　　机场客服代表
flight number　　　　　　　航班号

PART II *EMERGENCY PROCEDURES*

ground personnel	地服人员
ground operation	地面作业（部门）
cabin security check	客舱安全检查

Exercises

Please answer the following questions.

1. What are the three different types of threats an in-flight crewmember must be prepared for?
2. If a bomb is found on board the aircraft, what kind of procedures should the cabin crews follow?

Section 8   Hijacking

An important factor in handling a hijacking is to adopt a manner and attitude that will avoid alarming or frightening the hijacker or customers. All crewmembers must remain calm regardless of circumstances and must convey an air of calmness to others. The ability to remain cool, think straight, and operate calmly requires the knowledge of what to do under the given circumstances, and for this reason, procedural guidelines have been established.

When encountering hijacking, the flight attendant should advise the captain immediately. At some point during the flight, the hijacker will make known his desires. More than likely it will be a request or demand for access to the flight deck and/or conversation with the captain. Flight attendants must write down the demands in detail to ensure you relay the correct information and to buy some time and tell the hijacker access will be permitted only by interphone conversation and subsequent approval by the captain. Alert the flight deck of the situation, without alarming the hijacker or customers. To inform the captain of an attempted hijacker, you should attempt to move to the aft interphone, taking the hijacker with you. Call the captain via the interphone by ringing him twice. Advise the captain over the interphone by using the code word. Do not emphasize the code word and state it as though it were normal phraseology. This alert will provide the captain with sufficient warning to take certain actions during the time you escort the hijacker to the flight deck. The problem very quickly comes to rest primarily on the captain who must use his/her judgment and experience to bring about a successful and safe resolution of the threat. His/Her efforts will be aided by a team of support personnel on the ground, comprised of Flight Operations, company executives, and law enforcement authorities.

Captain will coordinate appropriate P.A. with "A" flight attendant. Customers should be advised of the situation and requested to stay seated with their seat belts fastened, remain calm and cooperate to the best of their abilities. It is suggested that crewmember must maintain control and keep flight deck continually informed. Slow down all of your actions. Delay, time is on your side. All the crew members should stay calm and set a good example for the customers. If necessary, individually assist, comfort and reassure customers. If conditions permit, establish rapport with the hijackers. All the crew should always remember the hijacker has a problem or they wouldn't be hijacking the aircraft. Consider them dangerous no matter what his/her mood is. If the hijacker does not speak or understand English, solicit other crewmembers or customers who may speak a language which the hijacker may understand. Have the selected person present the appropriate comment in that foreign language.

While dealing with the hijacker, retention of information is critical. Crewmembers should attempt to determine the hijacker's name and purpose for hijacking. Stay alert and observe the hijacker carefully to determine the following information: did the hijacker kidnap a specific individual? who did they kidnap and why? what/where the hijackers actions or reactions under various circumstances? was special cargo aboard? Obtain any other information which may be useful to authorities at a later date.

If there is any hijacking involving the presence of volatile mixtures, such as gasoline, poses a threat of flash ignition and explosion, causing possible structural or systems failure as well as casualties. In order to reduce or eliminate the possibility of such an occurrence, crewmembers must comply with the following:

–The "No smoking" sign will remain on and all customers should be instructed not to smoke cigarettes in order to eliminate a potential source of ignition.

–The flight deck door will remain closed so as to protect the flight crew from the effects of a flash fire and to reduce the charge of gasoline vapors getting into the flight deck where many sources of ignition are present.

–Request flight deck personnel to induce maximum air flow. In the event that a fire has started, air flow will be kept to a minimum.

–All crewmembers will be alerted to have Halon fire extinguishers ready in order to meet a fire problem early enough to keep it under control.

Do not make any written or verbal statements to the press or news media without prior briefing or approval from your airline's management.

Words and Expressions

emphasize ['emfəsaɪz]　*vt.* 强调；加强语气；重读
phraseology [ˌfreɪzɪ'ɒlədʒi]　*n.* 用语，措词；表达方式
hijack [haɪˌdʒæk]　*vt.* 劫持，绑架
comprise [kəm'praɪz]　*vt.* 包含，包括，由……组成
authority [ə'θɒrɪtɪ, ə'θɑr-]　*n.* 融洽；和谐
solicit [sə'lɪsɪt]　*vt. & vi.* 恳求，请求，乞求
retention [rɪ'tenʃən]　*n.* 具有，具备，享有，享用；挡住，拦阻；保持，容纳

kidnap ['kɪdˌnæp]   vt. 诱拐，绑架，劫持

volatile ['vɒlətaɪl]   adj. 易变的，反复无常的，易激动的

gasoline ['gæsəˌlɪn, ˌgæsə'lɪn]   n. 汽油

vapor ['veɪpə]   n. 水汽，水蒸气，无实质之物；自夸者

Technical Terms

flight deck	驾驶舱
Flight Operation	飞行运行（部门）
briefing	讲评

Exercises

Please answer the following questions.

1. When handling a hijacking, what abilities are required as a cabin crew?

2. When dealing with a hijacker, what should the cabin crew do?

3. Are the cabin crew allowed to make any written or verbal statements to the press or news media randomly?

PART ‖ *EMERGENCY PROCEDURES*

CHAPTER EMERGENCY EVACUATIONS

Section 1 Introduction

There are many factors that contribute to the successful evacuation of an aircraft. These include training, experience and behavior, the aircraft configuration, the layout of the cabin, the environment inside and outside the aircraft (e.g., the presence of smoke, fire, the cabin lighting, and outside conditions), the behavior of the passengers, their age, level of fitness and motivation.

During an emergency evacuation, it is essential for the cabin crew to be able to apply their knowledge of procedures, and rapidly adapt to the situation.

In the case of a life threatening situation on board the aircraft, it is essential that the aircraft is evacuated quickly and efficiently to increase the occupants chances of survival.

The role of the cabin crewmember will change from being customer service-oriented, to being a cabin safety specialist, an assertive leader, ready to act and in control of any given emergency situation.

Passengers rarely see this aspect of the cabin crew's role. During an emergency situation the passengers will look to the cabin crew for guidance and assistance.

The majority of emergencies that result in evacuation occur during the takeoff and landing phases of flight. They are frequently sudden and unexpected, or occur with very little warning. These types of emergencies leave crewmembers with little time to react.

Using Silent Review

The use of the Silent Review, or "the 30 second review", is an excellent tool to prepare for the unexpected. The "Silent Review" helps the cabin crew to focus their attention on safety. Crewmembers will also be ready to act, in the event of an unexpected emergency.

The constant use of the "Silent Review" is a key element in identifying emergency duties and responsibilities, and increases environmental awareness during the takeoff and landing phases of flight. It enables cabin crew to respond, adapt and react quickly in the event of an emergency.

"Silent Review" can take any form, and there are no hard and fast rules. It should contain all the elements needed to "Review" evacuation duties and responsibilities. It may include, but is not limited to, the following subjects: how to brace for impact; commands; cabin environment (identify under what circumstances cabin crew would initiate evacuation, fire, smoke, life-threatening situation, ditching, no response from flight crew); how to initiate evacuation, if necessary; operation of exits; alternate exits; how to assess outside conditions; self-protection; location of manual inflation handle; evacuation commands; location of able bodied passengers; location of passengers that require assistance, for example, disabled passengers, or unaccompanied minors.

Below is an example of a silent review used by some operators. It is easy to memorize. At the same time, this puts the order of the evacuation duties and responsibilities into prospective. This example is known as "**OLDABC**": operation of exits, location of emergency equipment, drills (brace for impact), able-bodied passengers and disabled passengers, brace position and commands.

The cabin crew should be alert to any indication that a possible emergency situation exists, when preparing for takeoff and landing. Such indications may be fire, smoke, scraping metal, unusual noises, the force of impact, or an unusual aircraft attitude.

Evacuation Commands To Passengers

The cabin crew must use positive verbal commands and physical gestures, in order to efficiently direct passengers towards the exits and assist them down the slides. Cabin crew must also be prepared to use some physical force, if necessary, to evacuate some passengers from the aircraft.

The commands used by the cabin crew should be assertive, positive, short, loud, clear and well paced.

There are many possible methods to alert the crew and the passengers, depending on their availability, such as public address, interphone, megaphone and evacuation alarm.

Words and Expressions

configuration [kənˌfɪgəˈreɪʃən]   n. 构造，形状，外貌，轮廓
layout [ˈleɪaʊt]   n. 布局；安排；版面设计
adapt to 变得习惯于……，使适应于……，能应付……
oriented [ˈɔːrɪentɪd,ˈəʊrɪentɪd]   adj. 以……为方向（目的）的，面向的
alternate [ˈɔːltəneɪt]   adj. 轮流的，交替的
                         n. 替换物；备用机场
brace [breɪs]   vt. 支持；使固定；使稳固；把……绷紧
scraping [ˈskreɪpɪŋ]   n. 刮屑；削片；（刮擦的）刺耳声
evacuate [ɪˈvækjuˌet]   vt.& vi. 撤离，疏散
assertive [əˈsɜːtɪv]   adj. 断定的；斩钉截铁的；过分自信的；武断的
pace [peɪs]   vt. & vi. 踱步于，走动；为……定步速（步调）
availability [əˌveləˈbɪlətɪ]   n. 可用性，有效性，实用性

Technical Terms

brace position   防冲撞姿态
unaccompanied minor(UM)   无成人陪伴儿童
silent review   （乘务员）静默程序回顾

Notes

1. The instruction to take the brace position will be the most important piece of

information that crew will give to passenger in an unplanned emergency. 在遇到无准备的紧急情况时,"做好防冲撞姿态"是乘务员给予乘客最重要的指令。

2. If an evacuation occurs away from an airfield, the cabin crew should take their assigned emergency equipment from the aircraft, if the situation permits. 如果撤离发生在远离机场的地方,在条件允许的情况下,乘务员要按照事先分配的任务携带应急设备离开飞机。

3. Directing passengers upwind and away from the aircraft. 指导乘客往机头方向跑,远离飞机。

注:撤离时,乘客应往机头方向跑,远离飞机至少 100 米。

Exercises

Please answer the following questions.

1. What does the roles of the cabin crewmembers play in an airplane?
2. What is the "Silent Review"?
3. What does the "OLDABC" mean?

Section 2 Unplanned Ground Evacuation

In the event of an "Unprepared Emergency", cabin crewmembers may only have enough time to give very short commands to prepare passengers for an imminent crash. In an unprepared emergency, the "Brace" command may come from the flight crew, or be initiated by the cabin crew.

The command to instruct passengers to assume the brace position, in any unplanned emergency will be "Heads down", "Hold your ankles", and "Stay down". The commands should be given until the aircraft has come to a complete stop. The instructions to take the brace position will be the most important piece of information that crew will give to passengers in an unplanned emergency. These commands must be repeated continuously, until the aircraft has come to a complete stop. This is to ensure that the passengers remain in the "Brace"

PART II EMERGENCY PROCEDURES

position, to maximize protection from injury.

Shout as loud as possible to be heard in the cabin. If possible try to synchronize calling commands, so that they come across loud and clear. Repeating the commands, even over a short period of time, is tiring for the voice. For this reason, it is important to try to alternate with another crewmember seated in the same area.

Unplanned Emergency Evacuation Procedures

All flight attendants should shout–"Heads down, Stay down!" This is to get the customer's head down. All crew continue shouting until the aircraft has come to a complete stop. There may be two impacts. Then stay in brace position until aircraft comes to a complete stop, and the captain will initiate an evacuation or direct the flight attendants to remain seated. If called upon to evacuate, each flight attendant should precede to his/her primary exit and assess outside conditions. If safe, open prior exit when shouting commands. If unsafe, block exit and proceed to secondary exit assignment. If proceeding to an over wing exit, ensure that your jump seat partner (if applicable) is informed of your intention. Continuing evacuation by using commands previously identified. In addition, "A" flight attendant will open the FWD entry door (conditions permitting), then place an ABP/ABA at that door to evacuate customers. The "A" position flight attendant then opens the FWD galley door (conditions permitting) and conducts the evacuation from that door. In addition, "B" flight attendant will turn on the EMERGENCY LIGHT SWITHC when the aircraft comes to a complete stop.

If it becomes necessary to use a secondary window exit, block your primary exit before proceeding down the aisle. If safe, open the window exit after assessment. Tell ABA to grab his/her seat cushion. Instruct ABA to attach the escape tape to the wing. Help people out and send them off the FWD edge of the wing. Add "Step out" to evacuation commands.

Unwarranted Evacuation

If a customer attempts (on their own initiative) to open an exit to evacuate the aircraft, the flight attendant should ascertain that there is no reason to evacuate (i.e. APU torching); shout the command "Stop", use the P.A. if immediately accessible; notify the flight deck and other crew members immediately; calm and reassure customers.

Exit Management

Monitor the progress of the evacuation, and ensure that the slide is clear at the bottom, and that there are no pile-ups. It is useful to ask two or three passengers to assist at the bottom of the slide. The crewmembers should use commands such as "Stay at the bottom", "Help people off" and "Send them away".

Passenger help at the bottom of the slide significantly reduces the risk of congestion and injury. Flight attendants should maintain the flow of the evacuation using commands such as "Jump and slide", "Form double lines (Dual lane slide)", "Form one line (Single lane slide)", "Keep moving" and "Hurry".

Crewmembers also need to be aware of any developments during the evacuation. For example, if the slide becomes damaged, or there is fire in the area, or anything that renders the exit unusable. The crewmember must "Stop" the evacuation at that door, "Block" the exit, and "Re-direct" passengers to the "Nearest usable exit".

When redirecting passengers, crewmembers need to be aware of which exit is usable to direct passengers to. Those who are in charge should also listen for another crewmember giving the command to "Come this way" or "Jump", indicating that the exit is usable. Then flight attendants redirect the passengers to the usable exit by using positive commands, such as "Blocked exit", "Go across", "Go forward" and "Go backward".

When the flow of passengers to the exit begins to slow down, the cabin crew should check the cabin and call all remaining passengers to the exits. When the flow of passengers has stopped, the cabin crew should check their assigned area for any remaining passengers.

If the cabin is in darkness, use a flashlight to check the cabin. Check the aisles, seats (including the floors area between the seats), galleys, lavatories, crew rest areas and cockpit.

When the cabin crewmember's assigned area is empty, or it is no longer safe to remain on board the aircraft, the cabin crewmember should evacuate through the first usable exit.

If an evacuation occurs away from an airfield, the cabin crew should take their assigned emergency equipment from the aircraft, if the situation permits.

Post Evacuation Procedures

The cabin crew will be responsible for a large number of passengers until the rescue and emergency services personnel assist them.

When the cabin crew have evacuated the aircraft they must manage the passengers on the ground. They should assist passengers away from the slides, direct passengers upwind and away from the aircraft. Keep passengers away from fuel fire and vehicles. Meanwhile, the cabin crew should assemble the passengers, keep them together and enforce no smoking. Prohibit the use of mobile phones. Assist passengers and give first aid when necessary. Make a passenger headcount, if possible. Flight attendant should obtain a first aid kit and a flashlight.

Cabin crewmembers seated near a megaphone should consider taking it from the aircraft to assist with crowd management post evacuation.

Words and Expressions

assume [ə'sju:m]　　vt. 假设，臆断，猜想；承担，担任，就职
maximize ['mæksə,maɪz]　　vt. 使……增加（扩大、加强）到极限
synchronize ['sɪŋkrə,naɪz,'sɪn-]　　vt. 把（钟表）拨至相同的时间；校准；（使）同步；（使）同速进行
detach [dɪ'tætʃ]　　vt. 拆卸，使分开，使分离
cushion ['kʊʃən] n. 垫子，坐垫
aisle [aɪl]　　n. 过道，通道
lane [leɪn]　　n. 航道；分道，跑道；泳道
pile-up 堆积；积聚
congestion [kən'dʒestʃən]　　n. 拥挤；堵车
render ['rendə]　　vt. 报答；归还；给予；呈递；提供；开出

blocked [blɒkt]　　*adj.* 封锁的，闭塞的，联锁的
lavatory [ˈlævəˌtɔrɪ, -ˌtərɪ]　　*n.* 厕所，盥洗室
vehicle [ˈvɪəkl]　　*n.* 交通工具，车辆
headcount　点人头数；总人数，职员总数
enforce [ɪnˈfɔːs]　　*vt.* 实施，执行；强迫，迫使
megaphone [ˈmegəfəʊn, ˈmɛɡˌfon]　　*n.* 扩音器

Technical Terms

unplanned evacuation　　　　　无准备的紧急撤离
over wing exit　　　　　　　　翼上出口

Notes

1. Stay in brace position until aircraft comes to a complete stop, and the captain will initiate an evacuation or direct the flight attendants to remain seated. 保持防冲撞姿态直到飞机完全停稳。机长依情况组织撤离或者指导乘务员保持坐在座席上。

2. Monitor the progress of the evacuation, and ensure that the slide is clear at the bottom, and that there are no pile-ups. It is useful to ask two or three passengers to assist at the bottom of the slide. 监控撤离的进展，保证滑梯下方无障碍，无乘客冲撞。寻找两名或者三名乘客到滑梯下方帮忙是有用的办法。

3. When the cabin crewmember's assigned area is empty, or it is no longer safe to remain onboard the aircraft, the cabin crewmember should evacuate through the first usable exit. 当乘务员所负责的区域已清空，或者留在飞机上已不再安全，乘务员应选择最近的可用的出口进行撤离。

4. Meanwhile, the cabin crew should assemble the passengers, keep them together and enforce no smoking. 与此同时，乘务员应该将乘客聚在一起，并强制执行不准吸烟的命令。

PART II *EMERGENCY PROCEDURES*

Exercises

I. Please answer the following questions.

1. What will be the most important piece of information that crew will give to passengers in an unplanned emergency?
2. When the flow of passengers has stopped in the dark cabin (no light), what should the cabin crew check in assigned area for any remaining passengers?
3. What should be done to manage the passengers on the ground after evacuation?
4. If the slide becomes damaged, or there is fire in the area or anything that renders the exit unusable, what should the cabin crew do?

II. Focusing on Practice

Objective:

　　Master the basic unplanned emergency evacuation procedures under different circumstances.

Suggestions:

1. Practice can be fullfilled through grouping in the class. All the process should be timed by the group leader or the instructor.
2. Practice can be situation-simulated. Learners can orally present the procedures or act out.

Section 3　Planned Ground Evacuation

　　A planned ground evacuation can be defined as an evacuation that enables the cabin crew to review procedures, and to inform and prepare passengers for an emergency landing. Crewmembers provide passengers with brace instructions, guidance on exit usage, and information on how and when exits should be operated. Effective communication between the crewmembers and the passengers is necessary for a timely, effective, and orderly response.

Cabin Crew Alert Phase

It is important for Operators to establish procedures in order to ensure that adequate guidance is provided to both flight crew and cabin crew on how to conduct abnormal and emergency briefings. For example, if the flight crew need to inform the cabin crew of an emergency, there may be a specific signal to alert the cabin, such as: a series of chimes; a specific phrase, i.e. "Purser to cockpit".

When crewmembers hear the signal, this indicates that an emergency situation exists, and that they must secure all equipment. Crewmembers should be ready, at their stations, to be briefed by the Purser via the interphone.

The Flight Crew to Purser Briefing

The flight crew should brief the Purser in a clear, precise and concise manner. The briefing should provide the Purser with the following information: nature of emergency (landing or ditching); time available to prepare the cabin (the cabin and flight crew should synchronize watches to assist with time management); what the brace signal will be; signal to remain seated (if no evacuation is required); special instructions/other information; who will inform the passengers and when (flight crew or Purser).

The Purser to Cabin Crew Briefing

The Purser will relay the information provided by the flight crew to all of the crewmembers. The Purser then will instruct the crewmembers to take their emergency checklists, take their emergency briefing position and be prepared for the emergency announcement and demonstration.

For psychological reasons, it is better for the flight crew to inform the passengers of an emergency. However, this may not always be possible, due to the workload of the flight crew during an emergency. Therefore, the Purser may be required to make the initial announcement. The Purser must explain the nature of the emergency and necessity to prepare the cabin and passengers must follow the instructions of the cabin crew.

Before the emergency demonstration begins, the cabin crew must ensure that the cabin dividers are open, the cabin lighting is turned up to 100% bright lighting and the entertainment system is switched off. The cabin crew should be ready to demonstrate the emergency briefing in their assigned areas.

Passenger Briefing

The aim of the briefing is to give passengers as much information as possible. The amount of time available will determine the extent of the briefing. Both passengers and crewmembers will need to give their undivided attention to the announcements. Therefore, there should be no elements of unnecessary distraction. This is the only opportunity that crewmembers will get to relate this information. To avoid distraction crewmembers should stay in the assigned brief/secure position and coordinate the demonstration with the announcement. The cabin crew should not walk up and down the aisle during the announcement or talk during the announcements.

When reading the safety briefing announcement, it is important to pause at key points, in order to give the cabin crewmembers time to demonstrate, and check passenger compliance.

The Contents of the Passenger Briefing

The brace position is essential when preparing passengers in an emergency landing. Reviewing the brace position during a passenger briefing will help to ensure that passengers are in the correct brace position for landing.

This position must be adapted if the seat is facing a seat back or a bulkhead or forward facing or aft-facing with a safety belt and a shoulder harness (crewmember seats only).

It must also be adapted if passengers are expectant mothers, traveling with infants or obese.

It must be emphasized to passengers that they should expect more than one impact, and they must remain in the brace position until the aircraft comes to a complete stop. The cabin crew must point out the "Brace" position on the safety information card, demonstrate holding/grabbing ankles/crossing arms and check "Brace" position and alternative "Brace" positions.

It is important to ensure that the passengers understand how to "brace" for impact correctly, to reduce injury. Passengers should press their backs into the seat. Seat belts should be worn as low and as tight on the torso as possible. The tighter the safety belt, the better the restraint is. Upper body should be bent forward as far as possible, with the chest close to the thighs and knees. Head should be down as low as possible. The head should be faced down in the lap. The head should not be turned to the side. Arms should be around or behind legs, tucked in against the body. Lower legs should be angled slightly behind the knee joints. Feet should be placed flat on the floor.

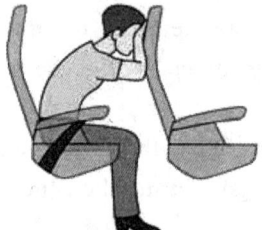

Figure 5.1

- Forward facing seat
- Safety belt only
- High density seating
- Against seat and against seat with break over feature

Figure 5.2

- Forward facing seat
- Safety belt only
- High density seating
- Against bulkhead

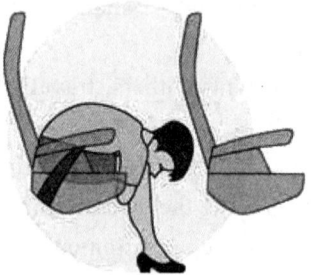

Figure 5.3

- Forward facing seat
- Safety belt only
- Low density seating
- Arms wrapped under legs

PART II EMERGENCY PROCEDURES

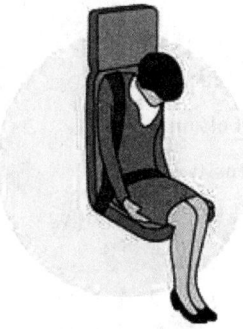

- Forward facing seat
- Safety belt and shoulder harness

Figure 5.4

- Aft facing seat
- Safety belt and shoulder harness

Figure 5.5

- Forward facing seat
- Safety belt only
- Low density seating
- Grabbing ankles

Figure 5.6

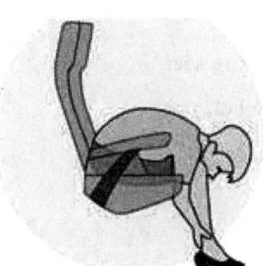

- Forward facing seat
- Safety belt only
- High density seating
- Against seat and against seat with break over feature
- Pregnant

Figure 5.7

・ 135 ・

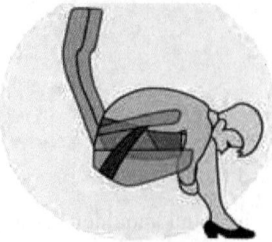

- Forward facing seat
- Safety belt only
- Low density seating
- Arms wrapped behind legs

Figure 5.8

- Aft facing seat
- Safety belt only

Figure 5.9

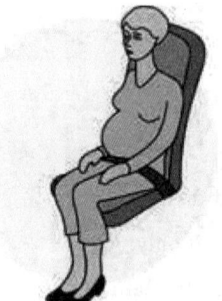

- Aft facing seat
- Safety belt only
- Pregnant

Figure 5.10

- Forward facing seat
- Safety belt only
- High density seating
- Adult holding infant

Figure 5.11

Standard Brace Position (Adult and Child)

−Seat belt securely fastened.

−Lean forward with feet flat on floor.

−Place head face down in lap.

−Wrap arms under knees.

Over Wing Aft Facing Seat Standard Brace position (Adult and Child)

−Seat belt securely fastened.

−Sit straight up.

−Head and back flush to seat.

−Hands placed under thighs.

Alternate Brace Position (Adult)

−Seat belt securely fastened.

−Feet flat on floor.

−Cross your wrists and place them on the seat back in front of you.

−Rest your forehead on the seat back.

Customer with Small Child

−Seat belt securely fastened.

−Lean forward with feet flat on floor.

−Wrap one arm under knee and place one arm over child or place one arm on seat back in front of you, forehead resting on seat back and one arm over child (lounge area).

−Child assumes forward facing seat bracing position.

Customer with Infant

−Forward facing seat.

−Safety belt only.

−High density seating.

−Adult holding infant.

If a car seat is available, instruct customer to leave infant properly secured in car seat. Advise customer to remove child from car seat when evacuating.

Illustrated Brace Positions

Once the brace position has been explained, the next step is to inform the passengers when to assume the brace position, for example:

"When you hear the crew shouting 'Brace, Brace, Brace', this will be your signal to take the 'brace position'. You must remain in this position until the aircraft has come to a complete stop."

Securing Loose Items

Passengers should remove and stow all loose sharp items from themselves, and secure them in an overhead bin, closet or under a seat. These objects include carry-on baggages, high heeled shoes, handbags, laptops and briefcases.

All of these items must be placed in an overhead bin, closet or under a seat. High-heeled shoes and sharp objects must also be removed, because these objects can cause damage to the slide during an evacuation. In addition, these objects must not be stowed in seat pockets, since they may injure passengers when they take the brace position.

Seat pockets should only be used to stow small objects, such as pens and eyeglasses. Cabin crew should also remove items such as pens, badges and wing pins from their uniforms.

Emergency Exit Location

The cabin crew must indicate the location of the nearest emergency exits and the floor proximity exit path lighting to the passengers.

Able Bodied Passengers

The International Civil Aviation Organization (ICAO) defines Able Bodied Passengers (ABPs) as "passengers selected by crewmembers to assist in managing emergency situations if and as required". The selection of ABPs is based on their ability to understand instructions, their physical ability, and their ability to stay calm. The ideal candidates are people such as: deadheading crewmembers; military personnel; police; fire personnel.

Ideally, crewmembers should select 3 ABPs at each exit. One of the ABPs should be briefed on the following.

–How to replace crewmembers in case they become incapacitated. However, crewmembers must emphasize that ABPs will replace crewmembers only if they are not able to perform their function due to incapacitation;

–How to assess conditions outside the aircraft, for example, how to identify that an exit is usable/no longer usable;

–How to open the exit;

–How to protect oneself from going overboard, to remain in the assist space and to hold on to the frame assist handle;

–Commands to be used during evacuation. i.e. "Jump and slide";

–How to open the crewmembers' seatbelt. The crew harness buckle is different from passengers' seat buckles, and a crewmember that is incapacitated in a crew seat may block a usable exit.

The two other ABPs should be briefed on how to assist the cabin crew during the evacuation, for example: holding passengers back during door opening and slide inflation; remaining at the bottom of the slide during the evacuation to assist other passengers.

The cabin crew should brief the ABPs seated at over wing exits on the following:

–How to assess the outside conditions;

–When to open the exit;

–How to open the exit;

–Commands to be used. i.e. "Come this way", "Step out", "Follow the arrows", "Run and slide";

–How to redirect passengers if an exit is no longer usable or blocked.

ABPs should also be assigned to assist passengers with special needs, such as: passengers with reduced mobility; the elderly; unaccompanied minors; people traveling alone with more than one child.

Final Cabin Secure Check

When the passenger briefing has been completed, the final cabin secure is required, as follows: seat belts fastened; seat backs in the up-right position; tray tables closed and latched; armrests down; carry-on baggage stowed and secured; overhead bins closed and latched; aisles clear of all obstructions; service items cleared; cabin dividers open.

Secure Galleys

When the passengers and the cabin have been secured, areas such as lavatories and galleys need to be correctly secured. All lavatories should be vacated and locked. All galley equipment should be stowed and secured. Close and lock all containers. Ensure that carts are correctly stowed and secured. Switch off all galley power and pull all galley circuit breakers.

Purser to Captain

When the cabin has been secured, and the cabin preparation is complete, the Purser will notify the flight crew. The Purser should also ask the flight crew for an update of the situation, and the amount of time remaining.

Back at Station

The cabin lighting should be adjusted according to the expected outside conditions. Cabin crewmembers should take their seats, adjust the harness, begin a "silent review", and be prepared to "brace", when the command comes from the flight crew.

There may be more than one impact. Therefore, remain in the "Brace" position until the aircraft stops. The aircraft must be at a complete stop before initiating an evacuation. Before opening a door forward, or aft of an engine, ensure the engines are not running. Evacuation should begin immediately upon receiving the "Evacuation Signal". "Positive Assertive" action from the cabin crewmembers will directly impact the rate of flow, and accelerate passenger movement to the exits and down the slides. The flight attendant should monitor the flow of the evacuation, and be aware of congestion in the aisles, and at the bottom of the escape slide. Be alert to evolving situations, for example, fire, or slide damage. Be ready to redirect passengers to another exit.

Post-evacuation

The majority of emergency evacuations happen at, or near, an airport. While the crewmembers are evacuating the aircraft, the Airport Emergency Plan

PART II EMERGENCY PROCEDURES

(AEP) is implemented. This plan consists of deploying emergency services such as Airport Rescue Fire Fighting, ambulances, and police to the scene.

The crewmembers are responsible for the passengers, until they are relieved by the rescue services. They must assist passengers away from the slides and direct the passengers away from fuel, fire and vehicles. Assist in marshalling passengers to a safe area upwind, away from the aircraft. Keep passengers together and complete a headcount. Treat injured passengers, and give first aid, if necessary. Enforce a "No smoking" policy.

Crewmembers should also receive training and survival information according to regions, such as: desert areas; tropical areas; Polar Regions; mountainous areas.

Words and Expressions

chime [tʃaɪm]   vt. & vi. 敲出和谐的乐声；报（时）
brief [brɪf]   vt. 向……介绍基本情况，作……的摘要
psychological [ˌsaɪkəˈlɒdʒɪkəl]   adj. 心理的；精神的
demonstration [ˌdemənˈstreʃən]   n. 表明；证明；示范
compliance [kəmˈplaɪəns]   n. 服从，听从，顺从
bulkhead [ˈbʌlkhed]   n. 舱壁，隔板；隔墙
impact [ˈɪmˌpækt]   n. 影响，作用
                   vt. & vi. 对某事物有影响
knee joint 膝关节，弯头结合，肘接
thigh [θaɪ]   n. 股，大腿
lean [liːn]   vt. & vi. （使）倾斜，屈身
lounge [laʊndʒ]   n. 休息厅，休息室；客厅
                   vi. 懒散地斜倚（靠坐）
illustrate [ˈɪləˌstreɪt, ɪˈlʌsˌtret]   vt. 说明，阐明；表明
laptop [ˈlæptɒp]   n. 便携式电脑
vacate [ˈvəˌkeɪt, veˈket]   vt. 空出；退出；腾出；撤离

deadhead ['dedhed]　　*n.* 免费乘客，免费入场者
　　　　　　　　　　　vt. & vi. 优待……免费入场（乘车）
harness ['hɑːnɪs]　　*n.* 安全带
buckle ['bʌkl]　　*n.* 搭扣，扣环
deploy [dɪ'plɔɪ]　　*vt.* （尤指军事行动）使展开；施展；部署

Technical Terms

planned ground evacuation	有准备的陆地撤离
ICAO	国际民间航空组织
AFT facing seat	面向机尾方向的座位
FWD facing seat	面向机头方向的座位
brace position	防冲撞姿态
Airport Emergency Plan (AEP)	机场应急预案

Notes

1. A planned ground evacuation can be defined as an evacuation that enables the cabin crew to review procedures, and to inform and prepare passengers for an emergency landing. 有准备的陆地撤离指的是乘务员有准备时间静默撤离程序，并且通知乘客，让其做好准备，进行紧急迫降。

2. The brace position is essential when preparing passengers in an emergency landing. 在紧急迫降时，指导乘客做好防冲撞姿态是至关重要的。

3. It must be emphasized to passengers that they should expect more than one impact, and they must remain in the brace position until the aircraft comes to a complete stop. 乘务员必须向乘客强调，飞机在紧急迫降时将出现不只一次的撞击，乘客必须保持防冲撞姿态直到飞机完全停稳。

4. High-heeled shoes and sharp objects must also be removed, because these objects can cause damage to the slide during an evacuation. 高跟鞋和所有尖锐物品都必须取掉，因为这些物件在撤离时容易损坏滑梯。

5. The ideal candidates are people such as: deadheading crewmembers; military personnel; police; fire personnel. 最理想的援助者候选人是：加机组的乘务人员、军人、警察和消防人员。

PART Ⅱ EMERGENCY PROCEDURES

Exercises

Ⅰ. **Please answer the following questions.**

1. What's the procedure for planned ground evacuation?
2. What's the briefing content for the ABPs?
3. When the passenger briefing has been completed, what does the required final cabin secure check include?

Ⅱ. **Focusing on Practice**

Objective:
    1. Master the different ways of safety demonstrations, including the safety demonstration under normal situations and the brace position demonstration.
    2. Master the basic passenger briefing points.
Suggestions:
    Practice can be fullfilled through grouping in the class. All the process should be timed by the group leader or the instructor.

Section 4 Ditching

    The definition of ditching is "a deliberate emergency landing on water when the aircraft touches down under control". However, in commercial aviation this is a rare occurrance.
    A ditching, when executed correctly, is survivable. During a planned ditching the cabin crew have notice, and therefore, sufficient time to prepare the cabin, or to advise passengers to put on their life vests.
    The actions and response of the cabin crew, during a "ditching" or inadvertent water landing, will have a direct effect on the chances of survival. Wet drills and ditching exercises that form part of the cabin crew's initial training and further emergency training provide the cabin crew with invaluable

information, which helps them to react effectively, and improves their situational awareness skills in emergencies.

Unplanned Ditching

In any unprepared emergency the reaction of the cabin crewmembers will depend largely on their situational awareness skills.

When preparing for take-off and landing, the use of the "Silent Review" will heighten crewmembers' situational awareness skills, and prepare them for the unexpected. When departing or arriving to a destination that involves flying over water, some ditching information in the "Silent Review" should be included. Think about the extra information that will need to be given to passengers, for example, the use of equipment:

–What commands should be used?
–What should be looked for, when assessing conditions?
–What would determine the exits, usable/unusable?
–What equipment should be used?
–How to use the slide raft?
–What equipment to take?
–How to manage passengers in the water?
–How to manage passengers in the raft?

Aircraft Floating

The level of the water will determine whether the exit is usable or not. Exits that are below water, or seeping water at the sides, are not considered usable.

Use all exits above the water line. If the level of water is at the doorsill, evacuate passengers directly on the slide/slide rafts, and leave the slide/slide raft attached to the floor of the aircraft.

If possible, avoid evacuating passengers directly into the water, although sometimes there may be no other option.

It is possible that aircraft fuel, hydraulic fluid and oil have contaminated the water; swallowing or being in contact with these fluids can cause temporary loss of hearing, vision and produce nausea. Boarding a raft from the water can be a difficult task, someone who is covered in fuel and oil will be slippery and difficult to grasp from the water.

Low water temperatures may also pose a threat of hypothermia. The symptoms of hypothermia may start within 10 minutes.

If the water is cold it may cause panic and shock. Shock can place severe strain on the body and lead to cardiac arrest.

Those who are non-swimmers are very susceptible to incapacitation and drowning.

Be prepared to shout instructions regarding how to board the slide-raft. "Shoes off", "Board on hands and knees," "Go to the end", and "Sit down".

Over–Wing Exits

Over-wing exits are secondary exits during a ditching, because they are not equipped with slide/slide rafts. If the over-wing exits are usable, attach the lifeline, when installed, to the hook on the wing.

Instruct passengers to step on to the wing, inflate their lifejackets, and hold on to the lifeline. If circumstances permit, keep the passengers together on the wing until rescue arrives.

Planned Ditching

Planned ditching in commercial aviation is a rare occurrence; however, in other sectors of aviation ditching does occur and is survivable.

Cabin Preparation–Ditching Differences

Preparing the cabin for a ditching is similar to preparing the cabin for a land evacuation; however, there are a few differences.

Alert Phase

Unlike a planned ground evacuation, there will be no instruction to "remain seated" in the flight crew to purser briefing. In this case it will be necessary for everyone to evacuate the aircraft.

–Nature of the emergency

–Time available (check watch)

–Special Instructions

–Brace signal.

Passenger Briefing

The passenger briefing will take the same form as the "planned ground evacuation" briefing; however, the passengers will need more information due to the nature of the emergency, and the equipment required to survive.

The amount of time available will determine the level of preparation. The most important survival information should take priority, and other tasks should be accomplished as time permits: life vests, brace position, exits, ABP briefings, safety checks and final cabin preparation.

Cabin crewmembers must have their own life vest before commencing the briefing.

The cabin crewmembers should be in their designated brief and secure area, equipped and ready to commence the passenger briefing.

Cabin crewmembers should listen carefully to the announcement, and coordinate the demonstration with the instructions.

When reading the safety briefing announcement, it will be important to pause at key points, in order to give the cabin crewmembers time to don their life vests, demonstrate, and check passenger compliance.

Able Bodied Passenger Briefings

The criteria used for selecting Able Bodied Passengers (ABPs) for a ground evacuation applies to ditching. Ideally, select three APBs per exit, and seat them at the exit.

One ABP should be briefed to replace the cabin crewmember in case the crewmember becomes incapacitated. The crewmember should brief the passengers on.

–How to assess conditions outside the aircraft, and identify if the exit is usable/unusable (determined by water level)

–How to open the exit

—How to locate the manual inflation handle

—How to protect him/herself from going overboard, and remain in the assist space.

—The commands to be used during evacuation

—How to board the slide/raft

—How to disconnect the slide/raft

—How to cut the mooring line to release the raft from the aircraft.

ABPs two and three should be instructed to board the raft to assist passengers. One ABP should be instructed to go to the end of the raft. The other ABP should be instructed to stay in the middle of the raft to assist passengers to the far end. On some aircraft types, the rated capacity of the slide/ rafts is lower than the number of people on board (such as the A320/A321), a round raft is located in the cabin. ABPs two and three are responsible for the round raft.

These ABPs will be briefed how to:

—Take the raft to the exit

—Use the mooring line to attach the raft to a fixed part of the aircraft, for example, a passenger seat

—Launch the raft (the raft must be thrown outside the aircraft)

—Manually-inflate the raft, in case it does not inflate.

—"Pull the mooring line." Board the raft and distribute passengers evenly.

When the ABP briefing has been completed, the cabin crew should perform final safety check to ensure that all loose or sharp objects have been removed, and that the cabin is secure.

For the A320, during the final cabin preparation, the survival kit should be attached to the slide raft by attaching the lanyard, that is located forward of the door, to the hook on the survival kit.

Post Ditching

When the exits have been opened, crewmembers will be able to determine how to evacuate passengers to the rafts. If the water is at doorsill level, the passengers may board the slide/slide raft directly from the aircraft. The slide/slide raft should be left attached to the floor of the aircraft.

Passengers must inflate their life vests, when exiting the aircraft. Distribute passengers evenly on slide/slide rafts, to prevent capsizing. If the water level is too far away from the doorsill, detach the raft from the doorsill using the "disconnect handle". The raft will still be attached to the aircraft by the mooring line. Crewmembers should pull the mooring line in, to keep the slide/slide raft close to the door to evacuate passengers.

Cabin crewmembers will need to continue shouting commands, to speed up the evacuation. When boarding passengers into the rafts, ensure that the passenger count does not exceed the raft capacity. Monitor the flow at each exit, and be prepared to re-direct passengers to other rafts, in case there is congestion, or if the cabin conditions change (for example, unusable exits, rising water, aircraft sinking).

Before the cabin crewmembers leave the aircraft, check the cabin to ensure that all passengers and crew have evacuated. Remove assigned emergency equipment from the aircraft. Inflate life vest and evacuate the aircraft into the assigned slide/slide raft. If the slide/slide raft is still connected to the aircraft, pull the "disconnect handle". If the slide/slide raft is still connected to the aircraft by the mooring line, cut the mooring line to separate the slide/slide raft from the aircraft. Retrieve the survival kit attached to the lanyard.

Once separated from the aircraft, get clear and upwind of the aircraft, but stay in the vicinity of the aircraft. Stay clear of fuel contaminated water, in case the fuel ignites. Stay clear of any debris, which may damage the rafts. Locate other survivors.

If possible, there should be at least one crewmember per slide/slide raft. The crewmember should take the leadership role. The survival of the passengers depends on the crewmember's knowledge, and ability to use the available survival equipment, and the ability to cope with the hazards and hardship.

As soon as the raft is clear of the wreckage, the cabin crew should deploy the sea anchor. The sea anchor must be deployed in order to prevent the raft from drifting with the current. It is possible to drift over 160 kilometers in one day, therefore making it difficult to locate survivors.

When survivors have been found in the water, immediate action should be taken to get them on board the slide raft. Throw the heaving ring located on the raft to the survivor and pull them towards the raft.

When bringing survivors into the raft, it is important to ensure that the weight is evenly distributed to avoid the raft from capsizing. Boarding handles, or boarding steps, are usually located on the slide raft to assist survivors. Passengers should be boarded from the toe end of the slide/raft.

Some survivors may be injured, or too weak to board the raft, and may require assistance. This can be quite difficult; however, there are techniques that may make it easier. Below is an example of one such technique. Two people should hold the person under the armpits (not the arms). Push the person down into the water, and then pull as the buoyancy from the life vest pushes the person up again.

However, keep the person informed of every step of the rescue, so that he/she can cooperate! Once onboard the raft, all persons should keep their life vests until rescued. Remember that keeping the raft close to the ditching site will make location easier.

Words and Expressions

deliberate [dɪˈlɪbərət]   *adj.* 故意的，蓄意的；慎重的，深思熟虑的
inadvertent [ˌɪnədˈvɜːt(ə)nt]   *adj.* 粗心大意的，因疏忽造成的，非故意的
drill [drɪl]   *n.* 钻头
heighten [ˈhaɪtn]   *vt. & vi.* （使）变高，（使）增大，（使）变高
implement [ˈɪmplɪmənt]   *vt.* 使生效，贯彻，执行
　　　　　　　　　　　　n. 工具，器具，用具
seep [siːp]   *vi.* （液体）渗，渗透
doorsill [ˈdɔːˌsɪl, ˈdor-]   *n.* 门槛
swallow [ˈswɒləʊ, ˈswɑlo]   *vt. & vi.* 吞，咽
nausea [ˈnɔːziə, -ʒə, -sɪə, -ʃə]   *n.* 作呕；恶心；反胃
hypothermia [ˌhaɪpəˈθɜːmɪə]   *n.* 低体温
cardiac [ˈkɑːdɪæk]   *adj.* 心脏（病）的
lifeline [ˈlaɪfˌlaɪn]   *n.* 救生索
lanyard [ˈlænjəd]   *n.* 系索
wreckage [ˈrekɪdʒ]   （坠毁物）残片，碎片；残骸
current [ˈkɜrənt, ˈkʌr-]   *n.* 水流，气流
commence [kəˈmens]   *vt. & vi.* 开始

Technical Terms

over-wing exit　　　　　翼上出口
unplanned ditching　　　无准备的水上迫降
life line　　　　　　　　救生绳
sea anchor　　　　　　　海锚

Notes

1. The level of the water will determine whether the exit is usable or not. 水平面的高度决定出口是否可用。
2. Instruct passengers to step on to the wing, inflate their life jacket, and hold on to the lifeline. 指挥乘客上机翼，将救生衣充气，并抓紧救生绳。
3. When boarding passengers into the rafts, ensure that the passenger count does not exceed the raft capacity. 当乘客登上救生筏，确保乘客的数量不能超过救生筏的承载能力。

Exercises

Ⅰ. Please answer the following questions.

1. What is the procedure for planned ditching?
2. What is the procedure for unplanned ditching?
3. What should be paid attention to after ditching?

Ⅱ. Focusing on Practice

Objective:

　　1. Master the procedures for planned ditching.

　　2. Master the procedures for unplanned ditching

PART Ⅱ *EMERGENCY PROCEDURES*

Suggestions:

Practice can be fullfilled through grouping in the class. All the process should be timed by the group leader or the instructor.

Section 5   Commands

Brace Commands

Planned

–Captain will give Brace Command–"Brace, Brace, Brace" over the PA one minute prior to landing. All flight attendants will follow the Captain's brace command with: "Heads down!"–"Stay down!" repeated continuously until further instructions.

Unplanned

–Flight attendants will shout the Brace Command–"Heads Down", "Stay Down"–at the time it is apparent there is a definite problem.

Evacuation Commands

–The Captain will give the command–"Evacuate" or "Remain Seated". Flight attendants should not initiate an evacuation unless the flight deck is incapacitated or conditions dictate.

Remain Seated

When captain gives this command, the "A" Position flight attendant will:

–Remain seated until further instructions from the flight deck.

–If further instructions do not follow in a reasonable amount of time, ring the flight deck twice and coordinate with flight deck.

Evacuate Commands

When captain gives the command "Evacuate", all flight attendants will. Shout continuous commands during evacuation.

Flight Attendants Commands

–"Open your seat belt"

–"Come this way."

–"This way out."

–"Leave everything."

–"Jump." (door exits)

–"Step out." (window exits)

Smoke Filled Cabin	**Water Evacuation**
(Add to your commands)	(Add to your commands)
"Cover your nose and mouths."	"Remove seat bottom cushions."
"Get below the smoke."	"Hold on to the straps!"

Once evacuation has begun it may be necessary to instruct customers to:

–"Move away from the aircraft!"

–"Stay together in a group."

–"No Smoking!"

Exercise

Focusing on Practice

Objective:

Keep firmly in mind different commands.

Suggestions:

Practice can be fullfilled through grouping in the class. Learner can crosscheck through various ways.

Section 6 Flight Attendant Jump Seats and Exit Responsibilities

Each flight attendant is assigned a specific jump seat position and responsibility so that, in the event of an emergency evacuation, the flight attendant can quickly evacuate customers.

PART II EMERGENCY PROCEDURES

Flight Attendant Jump Seat Assignments

POSITION	JUMP SEAT ASSIGNMENT
A	Forward jump seat door side
B	Aft jump seat door side
C	Aft jump seat aisle side
D	Forward jump seat aisle side

All flight attendants will assume the appropriate bracing position for every takeoff and landing.

<u>Forward Jump Seat</u>

–Shoulder harness and seat belt securely fastened with seat belt tight and low across hips. Buckle in center of lap.

–Feet flat on the floor, out from under jump seat.

–Head resting against seat back.

–Sit on hands, palms up.

<u>Aft Jump Seat</u>

–Shoulder harness and seat belt securely fastened with seat belt tight and low across hips. Buckle in center of lap.

–Feet flat on the floor, out from under jump seat.

–Chin resting on chest.

–Sit on hands, palms up

<u>Inoperative Jump Seat</u>

If a jump seat becomes inoperative during flight, a flight attendant must sit in a customer seat closest to the assigned exit.

Flight Attedant Exit Responsibility

POSITION	PRMARY EXIT	SECONDARY EXIT
A	Forward entry door	Over wing window exit
B	Aft entry door	Over wing window exit
C	Aft service door	Over wing window exit
D	Forward service door	Over wing window exit

Secondary Exits

The over-wing window exits are listed as secondary exits; however, flight attendants must use good judgment and common sense in moving to another exit if their primary exit is blocked. Conditions inside and outside the aircraft must be assessed and will best guide the flight attendant on what action to take. Conditions such as smoke, fire or obstructions may make an exit unusable. This may require that the flight attendant or a customer selected by the flight attendant to block that exit. The flight attendant should evaluate their personal risk and use the first available exit as a secondary escape route if conditions dictate.

To Block an Exit

–Cross arm in from of chest

–Shout "EXIT BLOCKED"

–Shout "TURN AROUND" or use appropriate direction.

Words and Expressions

assume [əˈsjuːm]　　*vt.* 取得（权力）；承担，担任；假设，假定；呈现

hip [hɪp]　　*n.* 臀部

chin [tʃɪn]　　*n.*（尤指人的）颏，下巴

palm [pɑːm]　　*n.* 手掌，掌状物

dictate [dɪkˈteɪt]　　*vt.* 口述；命令，指示

Technical Terms

the assigned exit	指定出口
over wing window exit	翼上出口
entry door	左侧舱门
service door	右侧舱门

Notes

1. Each flight attendant is assigned a specific jump seat position and responsibility so that, in the event of an emergency evacuation, the flight

attendant can quickly evacuate customers. 每个乘务员都有指定的座位和相应的职责，以便在应急撤离时迅速地帮助乘客撤离。

乘务员职责的划分应该根据不同的机型、不同航空公司的要求来实施。在客舱服务和应急撤离时，乘务员的职责也会不同。

2. Conditions inside and outside the aircraft must be assessed and will best guide the flight attendant on what action to take. 乘务员必须对机内和机外的环境进行评估，它能指导乘务员采取最佳的措施。

Exercises

Focusing on Practice

Objective:

Master the different responsibilities of cabin crew.

Suggestions:

Practice can be fullfilled through grouping through the procedures. All the process should be timed by the group leader or the instructor.

CHAPTER 6 SURVIVAL

Generally speaking, there are four basic principles to survival—water, protection, location and food. The following context will be based on these four principles.

Four Principles to Survival

Water

Crewmembers will need to assess how much food and water is available, and rations them accordingly.

Water is the most important element. It is possible to live on just water for 10 days or more. When the water supply is limited and can not be replaced, it should be used efficiently. Fresh water supplies should be protected from being contaminated from seawater. At night, if water is in short supply, the canopy can be rolled up at the side to collect dew, by using a sponge or cloth. The amount of water available, and the amount of people and their physical condition, should be considered when rationing water.

If you have shelter, rain can be a blessing since it provides safe water for you to consume. Except in places like tropical forests where rain comes down like clockwork, you may not get much warning. As such, it's important to prepare ahead of time to collect rain so that you can go about your other survival tasks.

With rain, the key tactic is to have as many collection points as possible. This means placing as many containers out as possible and ensuring there is nothing between them and the sky. In addition, if you can fashion gutters out of bark, plastic, or other materials you can significantly increase the surface area for catching the rain.

If you don't have any containers, your next best bet is to look for naturally occurring containers where rain may have collected. This includes rock crevasses and fissures.

As a kid, you probably ate snow or bit in to icicles. Not so much because you were thirsty, but because it seemed like a treat. The problem with eating snow when you're doing it to survive is that it lowers your core body temperature. Something you want to avoid if shelter and warmth are not at your fingertips.

The proper technique involves collecting snow, the fresher and cleaner, the better, and then finding a way to melt it. If you have a fire or stove, melting it won't be an issue. If these two options are absent, but you do have some additional water of your own, you can blend the two in a bottle and then agitate the blend to melt the snow. To help the melting process, you can also place the container between layers of your clothing, but be sure it isn't directly in contact with your skin.

If the conditions are right, the morning will bring with it dew that you can collect. You'll have to be ready to go as the dew will eventually evaporate as the day progresses. First off, you'll need to gather materials that are absorbent such as T-shirts and socks. Dew collection is as simple as passing the materials over the surface of grass or rocks where the dew has formed. Then wring out the water in to your mouth or a container.

Saltwater is dangerous to drink as it causes your body more harm than good in large quantities. However, old sea ice is usually salt-free and therefore safe to drink. Typically, old sea ice is blue, brittle, and has rounded edges whereas new ice is gray, hard, and salty. As with snow described above, you need to melt the ice before you consume it.

Protection

The importance of a shelter can't be overstated. Even in non-freezing climates, a shelter that protects you from rain and allows you to rest can be the difference between life and death. Your site should have the following characteristics:

—Close to your signal and recovery site.

—Close to sources of food and water.

—Large and level so that you can lie down comfortably.

—Surrounded by enough materials so that construction doesn't require you to forage at great distances.

The ideal site will have a southern exposure if you're north of the equator and a northern exposure if you're south of it. These exposures maximize the optimal light and heat from the sun throughout the day. Build your shelter so that the entrance faces east which will result in the early-morning sun exposure.

Erect the canopy to prevent wind-chill hypothermia from affecting wet bodies. When the canopy is erected, all occupants will be protected from the elements.

Check the physical condition of all passengers and other crewmembers on board, and administer first aid as necessary.

Seasickness can be expected. The smell inside the life raft and loss of visual reference increase the risk of seasickness. Vomiting causes a serious loss of fluid. If available, seasickness pills should be distributed. However, if they are not available, occupants should be instructed to look at the horizon to have a visual reference.

Use the bailing bucket and the sponges from the survival kit, remove water from the raft. The floor of the raft should be kept as dry as possible.

Try to keep the raft clean and dry to prevent illness and infection.

The condition of the raft should be frequently monitored. If necessary, inflate the buoyancy chambers using the hand pump that is in the survival kit. The buoyancy chambers should be firm, but not too hard. Inflation should be checked regularly.

Building a shelter will be hard enough that you shouldn't also have to worry about surrounding hazards. Keep the following in mind when selecting a site.

—Avoid avalanche slopes.

—Avoid drainage and dry riverbeds with a potential for flash floods.

—If near bodies of water, stay above tide marks.

—Avoid rock formations that might collapse.

—Avoid dead trees that might blow down and overhanging dead limbs.

—Avoid animals and their trails.

Location

To maximize the effectiveness of a signal you need to use it at the appropriate time and in a good location. Use the following guidelines to select a proper signaling site.

–The site should be close to your camp or shelter.

–It should be located in the largest available clearing you can find.

–If possible, the site should have a view that extends 360 degrees.

–If no clearing is available, placing the signal next to a stream is a good alternative.

–Be careful to avoid shadows and overhangs so that your signal will not be obscured.

There are several types of rescue signals.

First, illumination and smoke flares. Flares can be very useful, but don't wait until you need a flare to become familiar with how to use one. Things will go a lot smoother if you study the instructions before finding yourself in a survival situation. Here are some general guidelines for using a signal flare. If practical, prepare your flare for use in advance, take care to keep it dry. When signaling for an air rescue, don't ignite the flare until the rescuer has been sighted approaching your direction. Since flares have the potential to burn you, always handle them with care and never point them toward yourself or someone else. It's best to hold them away from the body, at a 45 degree angle and pointing toward the ground. Be sure the bottom is not pointing toward your body as there have been incidents where flares have ignited out of the bottom, severely burning the operator. Most day flares emit a bright orange smoke that lasts approximately twenty seconds. For best results, use these flares on calm, clear days only. If the weather is bad, chances are that the smoke will dissipate before being seen. Most night flares emit a bright red flame that lasts approximately twenty seconds. For best results, use these flares at night.

Second, signal mirrors with sighting holes. On clear, sunny days, signal mirrors have been seen from as far away as 70 to 100 miles. Although such mirrors make for great signaling devices, they require practice to become proficient in their use. The following are instructions on using a commercial signaling mirror.

—Hold the signal mirror between your index finger and thumb of one hand. Reflect the sunlight from the mirror onto your other hand.

—While maintaining the sun's reflection on your free hand, bring the mirror up to eye level and look through the sighting hole. If done properly, you should see a bright white or orange spot of light in the sighting hole. This is commonly called the aim indicator or fireball.

—While continuing to hold the mirror close to your eye, slowly turn it until the aim indicator is on your intended target. If you lose sight of the aim indicator, start over.

—Since the mirror can be seen from great distances, it's a good idea to sweep the horizon periodically through the day even if no rescue vehicles are visible.

—When signaling an aircraft, stop flashing the pilot after you're certain he's spotted you, so that the flash doesn't impede his vision.

—When signaling from land, jiggle the mirror slightly to add movement to the signal.

—When at sea, hold the mirror steady so that it appears different than the sparkles created by the natural movement of the water.

Third, space blankets. These blankets have two sides with one being silver and the other being dark. In a snowy environment, place it in a clearing with the dark side up, since it will contrast nicely against the white snow. Otherwise, place the space blanket in a clearing with the silver side up. In either case, weigh down the edges, so it won't blow away. As you go about meeting your other survival needs, a well-positioned space blanket can be a passive, yet effective alert to potential rescuers of your location. The space blanket should be used as a signaling device ONLY when it's otherwise not necessary to meet more immediate survival needs such as staying warm and dry.

Fourth, whistles. With no moving parts, a whistle will never wear out and its sound travels father than the screams of the most desperate survivor. As such, always carry a whistle whenever you're out in the wilderness. As soon as you become lost or separated, begin blowing your whistle in multiple short bursts and repeat every 3 to 5 minutes. If rescue doesn't appear imminent, go about meeting your other survival needs while stopping periodically throughout the day to blow the whistle. It may alert rescuers of your location, even if you're unaware of their presence.

Food

The general rule is, "if you don't have water, don't eat". Only eat if water is available, as it is necessary to aid digestion.

Eating bugs may mean the difference between life and death in an extended survival situation. Not all bugs are safe to eat, so be careful in your selection. The following is a list of six edible bugs along with some tips on how to find them. As you'll see, you'll have the most luck surviving in forests which provide the necessary cover, food, and moisture that many bugs seek out.

–Insect larvae, also known as grubs, are not only easy to find, but they're easy to collect. They favor cool, damp places, so some good spots to look include in rotten logs, under the bark of dead trees, under rocks, and in the ground. Grubs are safe to eat raw, but of course you might find them more palatable cooked.

–Grasshoppers are also quite readily found, but they'll be a little more difficult to catch. Start by looking in open fields for the familiar chirping sound. Or just walk through a field and observe the kinds of insects that jump away from your feet. You can increase your chances by collecting them in the cool morning. Before eating a grasshopper, remove its legs because they are barbed and have the potential to get stuck in your throat. Grasshoppers should be cooked because they carry parasites.

–Ants can be found in just about all locations throughout the world. Their nests are generally in the ground and that is where you want to attempt to collect them. To start, disturb the nest with a stick. Instinctively, the ants will climb on to the stick to defend their home. As they do, dip the stick into a container of water so that the ants fall off the stick. Continue this process until you have collected an adequate supply of ants. Ants can be safely eaten raw or cooked. One caveat, if you are going to eat the ants raw, be sure they are dead first, otherwise they may bite you.

–If there is a damp meadow or forest close to your location, you may have some luck finding slugs. Some slugs are particularly big and so collecting sufficient numbers is much easier than with other bugs. Like grubs, slugs can be eaten raw or cooked with the cooked option making them far more appealing.

—You probably won't be able to distinguish maggots, which are the larvae of flies, from grubs, but they too are safe to eat raw or cooked. They favor damp places where decaying matter is abundant.

—Earthworms thrive in moist, warm soil, but you'll need to do a little digging to find them unless they've been forced out of the ground by rain. They can be eaten raw or cooked.

Unfortunately, many of the bugs you come across shouldn't be eaten even in a survival situation. Here are some guidelines for what to avoid.

—Bugs that are generally associated with carrying diseases should not be eaten. This includes flies, mosquitoes, and ticks.

—Some bugs use poison for capturing prey and for defense making them inedible, so avoid centipedes, scorpions, and spiders.

—As a general rule, bugs with fine hairs, bright colors, or eight or more legs are off limits.

You can actually sustain yourself quite well with bugs, so give them serious consideration when you're otherwise without food and trying to survive in the wilderness. They have the additional benefits over animals and fish of being plentiful, not requiring traps, and needing little preparation before they can be consumed.

Many plants are a viable food source, but they must be positively identified first to ensure they are safe to eat. There are four types of edible plants. Grasses can be easily located in meadows, drainages, and dry riverbeds. The stems, roots, and leaves may be eaten raw or cooked. In addition, a good broth or tea can be made by boiling grass in water. Black or purple grass seeds should be avoided as these colors indicate a fungal contamination, which when ingested can cause severe illness or death. Cattails can be easily located in swamps, marshes, and wet low-lying areas. The cattail has a stout stem from 6 to 9 feet tall, with leaves that are light green, lean, sword shaped, and frequently higher than the flower. The flower heads are dense, brown, and cylindrical. In spring, the young shoots and flower heads are the most edible portions and are best when peeled and eaten raw or dried and pounded into flour for later use. In late summer, the peeled roots are another source of flour when dried and pounded into a powder. Pine trees are prominent in many North American forests, easily identified as tall, multiple-branched trees with scaly bark and sharp evergreen needles arranging in bundles of two, three, or five. In addition, many have large, egg-shaped cones. Pine needles may be eaten raw or cooked, or they can be boiled in water to make a broth or tea. Pine tree needles also offer the additional benefit of being available year round. The cambium layer, between the bark and inner wood, may be eaten raw or cooked or can be dried and pounded into flour for later use. The seeds, located under the scales of the cones, may also be eaten raw or cooked although their small size means collecting a lot of pine cones. Common green seaweed can be easily located on both sides of the Pacific and Atlantic Oceans. Be warned that seaweed found on the beach tends to contain mold so it is best to choose plants that are attached to rocks or floating free. Seaweed may be eaten raw or dried until crisp and used in soup or broth.

In general, the edibility of berries can be classified according to their color and composition. The following are guidelines to help you determine whether a berry is poisonous. These rules do guarantee edibility–only positive identification can do that.

–Green, yellow, and white berries are 10 percent edible.

–Red berries are 50 percent edible.

–Purple, blue, and black berries are 90 percent edible.

–Aggregate berries, such as thimbleberries, raspberries, and blackberries are 99 percent edible.

Many plants have distinguishing characteristics that once identified can be used as signals for what not to eat. The six basic features of plants that are likely to be detrimental to your health are mushroom or mushroom like appearance, umbrella-shaped flower clusters, bulbs resembling onion or garlic, carrot-like leaves, roots, or tubers, bean and pea-like appearance and plants with shiny leaves or fine hairs.

Obviously many safe plants have characteristics that match those described above. The key to remember is that a similar appearance to a known safe plant doesn't make that plant safe to eat.

Signal for Help

Signaling indicates that you need help and many of the methods of signals are a universal language, recognizable all over the world. There are so many methods of creating a distress signal that it all depends on what materials you have available.

If you are in trouble you can use visual or audio signals to indicate your position. Visual signal types are the most efficient ones and there are many ways you can signal for help using these methods.

Using a shiny surface to signal for help. This is probably the easiest method to signal for help and it involves using a mirror or any shiny surface to create a flash. This method can be useful if there are people in your vicinity or if a plane or helicopter is fling by. You have to reflect the sunlight onto your hand and then position your hand so that it covers the target in your field of vision. Remove your hand and wobble the mirror back and forth. You can signal for help using any type of shiny object, but you should also have other alternatives to signal for help.

Using Fire to signal for help. If you are in the woods, you can use rocks or branches to spell out "S.O.S", the international code for "save our souls" that is recognized all over the world as a signal for help. You can also look for a clearing and make big fire. This will definitely attract the attention of people from a far. You need to make a fire as big as you can to signal for help and this will require a lot of work. You have to gather a lot of wood and burnable material so that you can keep it going for a long time. If you are running out of time and you cannot gather a lot of burning material, you can light three fires in a straight line or in a triangular pattern. Anyone that sees this formation will understand that is not a random fire and in fact, it's a signal for help. You can increase the visual effect of the fire by putting green branches on it. This will create a lot of smoke that can be seen from a long distance. Make sure you stand downwind to avoid inhaling the smoke.

Using flares to signal for help. If luck is on your side, you could have brought a couple of flares with you. This will bring you a great advantage as long as you know how to use and ration them. You have to signal for help only when you hear something in the distance, such as a helicopter. Never set more than one

PART ‖ EMERGENCY PROCEDURES

flare at a time. If a plane passes by and sees your flare, the pilot will rock the plane from side to side, to let you know your signal for help has been seen. Of course that things change at nighttime, so you just have to wait and see if the rescuers find you. You can signal for help using another flare if you hear any sound that might come from a rescue party, such as a whistle or aircraft sounds.

Using a flashlight to signal for help. A flashlight can do wonders at night if you need to signal for help and it is the only thing you've got. A flashlight can also be used in heavily shaded areas. If you need to use the flashlight to signal for help, you have to make a choice and use the batteries only for flashing purpose. Don't wander at night and keep in mind to conserve your energy and your light accordingly. When you signal for help using a flashlight, you have to keep the same pattern, three small flashes at the time. In order to make the S.O.S. code with a flashlight you have to do this: three quick flashes, three long flashes, three short flashes then a pause.

Using a whistle to signal for help. Most of us carry a whistle when we go in the woods and it's a must have item for any bug out bag. Although it's not as successful method as a visual sign, sometimes it can be your only option to signal for help. You have to remember that when you use the whistle you have to do it in burst of three. This is recognized as a signal for help and chances are someone will hear it. Don't wear yourself out and take breaks. You will have to pay attention and drink some water because you lose saliva when you blow the whistle and you will become dehydrated when you signal for help.

Using bright colors to signal for help. When you are lost or trapped somewhere and you hear a plane approaching your location, don't start to jump about and scream because you will only get tired. While motion can be okay when you need to signal for help, yelling or screaming is pointless because the pilot of the plane can't hear you. You will end up wearing yourself out. What you should do instead is to take off the most brightly colored piece of clothing you have and wave it around. This will certainly attract the attention and you will be less tired when you signal for help. However, this is not all, you can also leave markings using bright colors, you can tie pieces of clothes on the trees or if you have a permanent marker in your bug out bag, you can use it to write "Help!" on anything from trees to rocks. Using bright colors to signal for help is widely used when there are floods or any other type of natural disasters that prevent people from leaving their homes. Using bright colors to signal for help is a good method, regardless the environment you're in.

Rescue

When an aircraft or a ship has been sighted, all the signaling equipment available should be used to attract attention. Occupants must stop signaling as the craft approaches.

Do not attempt to swim unless it is for a very short distance. A general rule of thumb to remember is that a strong swimmer has a 50-50 chance of surviving a 50-yard swim in 50-degree water. The only reason to swim is if safety is close by or if there's an object that will make it easier for you to remain afloat. Try to remain still to keep your heart rate low. And of course, breathe normally.

If you are alone and wearing a flotation device, there's a position you should take to reduce your heat loss by up to 50%. Cross your ankles, draw your knees to your chest, and cross your arms over your chest. Keep your hands high on your chest or neck to keep them warm. Do not remove your clothes as they will not weigh you down, but they will provide some warmth by holding warm water close to your skin.

If there are other people in the water with you and everyone is wearing a flotation device, gather together and "hug" with chests touching chests. The closeness will help you share heat and also has the side benefit of making you more visible to rescuers.

If you aren't wearing a life jacket, the same rules apply. However, seek out debris to help you float. If nothing is available, you can float on your back or tread water slowly. As a last resort, you can attempt to fill your jacket with air from the bottom. Be warned that this sort of movement can hasten the cooling of your body.

Passengers and crewmembers will have to be patient during the rescue operation, and understand that the procedure takes time, depending on the type of rescue craft. The crewmember will need to manage the passengers calmly, and maintain order until the last person has been rescued. The crewmembers and

PART Ⅱ EMERGENCY PROCEDURES

passengers must follow the instructions of the rescue personnel and remain until instructed.

  With modern satellite technology, location and rescue may not be far away. However, it is always best to prepare for the most extreme circumstances. Crewmembers should feel confident that their knowledge and survival techniques would get them through the worst possible circumstances. Crewmembers are always the leaders in any emergency situation. An effective leader has knowledge and skills, plus the ability to apply those skills as necessary.

Words and Expressions

ration ['ræʃən, 'reʃən]   *vt.* 限量供应；配给供应
                          n. 定量；配给量
contaminate [kən'tæməneɪt]   *vt.* 把……弄脏，污染
clockwork ['klɒk،wɜːk]   *n.* 钟表机构，发条装置
tactic ['tæktɪk]   *n.* 方法，策略
crevasse [krɪ'væs]   *n.* 破口，崩溃处，裂缝
fissure ['fɪʃə]   *n.* 狭长裂缝或裂隙
imminent ['ɪmɪnənt]   *adj.* 迫切的，危急的，逼近的，即将临头的
larva ['lɑːvə]   *n.* 幼虫，幼体
grub [grʌb]   *n.* 蛴螬，蛆
rotten ['rɒt(ə)n]   *adj.* 腐烂的；腐朽的
palatable ['pælətəbəl]   *adj.* 可口的，美味的
grasshopper ['grɑːs،hɒpə]   *n.* 蚱蜢
chirp [tʃɜːp]   *vi.* 鸟叫；虫鸣
detrimental [،detrɪ'ment(ə)l]   *adj.* 有害的，伤害的
be detrimental to 对……不利的，对……有害(to)
cluster ['klʌstə]   *n.* （果实、花等的）串，簇
resemble [rɪ'zemb(ə)l]   *vt.* 像……，类似于
tuber ['tuːbə, 'tjuː-]   *n.* 块茎，球根
vomit ['vɒmɪt]   *vt. & vi.* 呕吐
chamber ['tʃeɪmbə]   *n.* 房间

transceiver [træn'si:və]　　*n.* 收发设备；无线电收发（两用）机
morale [mə'rɑ:l]　　*n.* 士气；斗志
cramped [kræmpt]　　*adj.* 受拘束的，紧缩的，狭窄的；难懂的，难读的；
　　　　　　　　　　　　　难认的

Exercises

Please answer the following questions.

1. What are the four basic principles to survival?
2. How can you get water source?
3. What are the rules for selecting a proper signaling site?
4. How do you use a signal mirror?
5. What types of plant do one need to avoid eating?
6. What are the suggested ways for protection on sea?
7. What's the method for you to share heat with others in water?

REFERENCES

[1] Airbus 320 CCOM[Z]. Airbus Industry, 2006.

[2] GREGORY J DAVENPORT. Wilderness Survival[M]. Mechanicsburg: Stackpole Books, 1998.

[3] CHRIS TINE SIRONCK, CHRISTOPHE ADANI. Cabin Smoke Procedures[EB/OL]. [2012-09-08] http://www.airbus.com/fileadmin/media-gallery/files/safety-library-items.

[4] Flight Operation Briefing Notes[Z]. Airbus Industry, 2006.

[5] Flight Operation Briefing Notes[Z]. Airbus Industry, 2007.